CW01302465

THE PERILOUS ROAD TO ROME VIA TUNIS

THE PERILOUS ROAD TO ROME VIA TUNIS

Edward Grace MC

Foreword by Lieut-General Sir Peter Graham, KCB, CBE

PARAPRESS LTD
Tunbridge Wells

© Edward Grace 1993
ISBN 1-898594 06-6

First published in the UK in 1993
PARAPRESS LTD
12 Dene Way
Speldhurst
Tunbridge Wells
Kent
TN3 0NX

British Library Cataloguing in Publication Data:
A catalogue record for this book is available
from the British Library

Printed in Great Britain by
Ipswich Book Co. Ltd., Ipswich,

All rights reserved. No part of this
publication may be reproduced,
stored in a retrieval system or transmitted in
any form or by any means,
electronic, mechanical, photocopying,
recording or otherwise,
without prior permission in writing from
Parapress Ltd, publishers.

Contents

Foreword by Lieut General Sir Peter Graham, KCB, CBE   1
Author's Preface   3

PART I – TUNISIA

1. Operation Torch – to Tunis   7
2. The Attack   16
3. Minefields and Tanks   23
4. The Awesome Bou Aoukaz   29
5. Montgomery v Rommel   37
6. The Final Offensive   41
7. Victory!   47
8. Twelve Thousand Prisoners   55
9. Après Guerre   61
10. Christmas in the Italian Hills   70

PART II – ANZIO

1. The Prelude   75
2. Churchill's Wild Cat   86
3. The Advance of the Guards' Brigade   95
4. Horror Farm   105
5. Epic Battles   122
6. Backs to the Wall   128
7. The German Offensive   143
8. My Turn Next?   157

Epilogue   162

Maps

1	The Battles of Banana Ridge, Longstop and Bou Aoukaz	17
2	Line up of troops before final offensive	42
3	German Gustav Line January 1944	78
4	Allied landing, Anzio beach-head, 22 January 1944	81
5	Guards Brigade attack	96
6	6th Gordons at Horror Farm	106
7	US Darby Rangers Battle	125
8	German Offensive 18 February	144

Bibliography

Alexander, Lord. *War in the Cruel Mountains* (Sunday Times, 1961)
Churchill, Winston. *Second World War* Vol V (Cassell, 1952)
Clifford, Alexander. *Three against Rommel* (Harrap, 1943)
D'Este, Carlo. *Fatal Decision* (Harper Collins, 1991)
Horrocks, Lt-General Sir Brian. *A Full Life* (Collins, 1960)
Kesselring, Field Marshal Albert. *Memoirs* (William Kimber)
Majdalany, Fred. *Cassino, Portrait of a Battle* (Longmans, 1975)
Marshall, Howard. *Over to Tunis* (Eyre & Spottiswoode, 1943)
Moorehead, Alan. *The End in Africa* (H Hamilton, 1943)
Moran, Lord. *Winston Churchill, The Struggle for Survival* (Constable, 1966)
Vaughan-Thomas, Wynford. *Anzio* (Longmans, 1961)
Williamson, James. *6th Gordons 1939-45* (Aberdeen Press & Journal)
Wilson Guthrie (ed). *Gordon Highlanders in Picture 1940-45*

Foreword by
Lieutenant General Sir Peter Graham KCB CBE
Colonel, The Gordon Highlanders

It is with real pleasure that I write this Foreword to *The Perilous Road*. My generation does realise what a huge debt we owe our fathers' generations which volunteered for and took part in the war against Nazi Germany, Fascist Italy, Imperial Japan and their Allies. That the outcome of that war was successful was in no small way due to the commitment, leadership and courage of young officers. These are the men who lead at the sharp end of the fighting. Ted Grace, a young Platoon Commander in B Company of the 6th Battalion, The Gordon Highlanders, was one of those. The book is also about the exploits of that Battalion of my Regiment, a Battalion in which my father-in-law served as a young officer from 1936-1940 until he was captured by the Germans during the Fall of France.

But who are The Gordon Highlanders? The Gordon Highlanders – one of Scotland's most famous infantry regiments – were raised in 1794 by the Duke of Gordon to fight in the Napoleonic Wars. The Regiment served with great distinction in Wellington's Peninsular Campaign when Napier wrote of them that their 'stern valour would have graced Thermopylae'. The Regiment served at Waterloo where they took part in the famous 'Scotland For Ever' charge with the Scots Greys. The Gordons often served on the North West frontier of India in the days of the Raj. In 1880 they marched with Lord Roberts from Kabul to Kandahar, leading the successful assault on that city. Later in 1897 they won worldwide renown for their courage at Dargai when they took the Afridi's positions which three other regiments had failed to do. Piper Findlater who had continued to play his pipes whilst under fire and having been severely wounded, won the VC. Winston Churchill described the Regiment during the Boer War as 'the finest Regiment in the world'. In both World Wars, The Gordon Highlanders were awarded battle honours including El Alamein, Goch and Anzio. They have served with distinction since 1945 in Malaya, Cyprus, Borneo and Northern Ireland; indeed as I write, a platoon of the 1st Battalion is serving in Bosnia.

The year 1994 will be important in two respects; it is the 200th Anniversary of the raising of The Gordon Highlanders and the 50th Anniversary of the Allied Landing on the Anzio beach-head leading to the fall of Rome. It seems to me therefore that it is particularly appropriate that this history should be published now.

'History' the very word can sound dull, but this is not a dull book. It reads so easily, is exciting and is just like an adventure story – which of course it is and a true one. Ted Grace captures the challenge and excitement that he felt as a young man leading his Jocks. It is a wonderful description of life as a young Platoon Commander in a busy, active Battalion and one that shows the need for, and the results of, first class leadership at a junior level. It shows the concerns, fears and worries of a brave and dedicated young man. There is much for our modern youngster to learn from this book and I commend it to them most strongly and indeed to every military officer. It also shows the huge sacrifice that was made on our behalf so that we have the freedom which we value so highly.

Ted Grace has also captured the character and spirit of the Gordon Jock, greatly envied by other regiments in the Scottish Division. The North East of Scotland – Aberdeenshire, Banffshire and Kincardineshire, produces wonderful soldiers. The Gordon Highlanders are simply a reflection of the character of that special part of Scotland.

Perhaps one of the best recent testimonies concerning the Regiment has come from Brigadier David Bromhead whose ancestor won a VC at Rorke's Drift. In July 1993 he wrote to the Colonel in Chief, His Royal Highness The Prince of Wales, saying of the 1st Battalion which was serving under his command in Berlin, 'They are an outstanding Battalion, tough, fit and disciplined. Their time in Berlin has been an unqualified success. I know all amalgamations are tough but their pending disappearance is particularly sad. They are an exceptional Regiment.'

Let us pray that amalgamation does not come about so the real spirit of such a splendid Regiment, so aptly described in this book, can remain undiluted and unchanged.

Preface

Britain in 1943 was a land of contrasts. Having survived Dunkirk and the Battle of Britain, and having endured months of intensive bombing and the ever-present threat of invasion, the people had become accustomed to austerity and hardship, and to families being separated, children evacuated, rationing, the black-out and innumerable restrictions.

Yet the country was healthy, used to keeping fit, digging for victory, fire-watching, and doing without luxuries. As a result, crime was almost unknown, and the national pride was centred around the well-loved King George VI and Queen Elizabeth.

Britain was also a country of companionship; every person was a friend. Men and women in all walks of life were united in the belief that it was our destiny to uphold the future of civilisation against the forces of evil. From the General in Whitehall, the soldier, sailor and airman, to the girl serving soup in the kitchen and the old woman making socks and scarves for the troops, all were equally involved and equally patriotic.

This book begins in February 1943, when as a young Lieutenant in B Company of the Sixth Battalion of the Gordon Highlanders, I spent months of training and manoeuvres with the First Division in Scotland before being sent on embarkation leave and then departing from Liverpool on a long naval convoy to Algiers as part of Operation Torch. Our troop-ship was the once beautiful liner the *Duchess of Argyll*. Although we arrived unscathed, we later learnt that on its return voyage the ship was torpedoed and sunk. Other ships in our convoy were also sunk by bombs and U-boats. As a result, we lost many tanks, trucks and heavy equipment which took about ten weeks to replace.

The war at that time was at a critical stage. In the Battle of the Atlantic the U-boats were strangling our life-line. Everything on land, at sea and in the air depended on our defeating this menace. In March 1943, 120 ships, being nearly 700,000 tons of shipping, were sunk in spite of the indomitable bravery of those at sea. As Winston Churchill wrote, 'Many gallant actions and incredible feats of endurance are recorded, but the deeds of those who perished will never be known. Our merchant seamen displayed their highest qualities and the brotherhood of the sea was never more strikingly shown than in their determination to defeat the U-boat.'*

In the Far East the American Navy had proved superior to the Japanese. In November 1942, in a fierce running battle lasting two days, a Japanese battleship, a cruiser, three destroyers and seven troop transports were sunk at a cost to the Americans of only one destroyer. As a result, the airbase of Guadalcanal in the Solomon Islands was finally captured, thus inflicting a severe defeat on the Japanese. The tide of war in New Guinea was also turning in our favour, just as the American-Australian air-power was fast increasing.

A significant feature of the war at that time was the friendship and understanding between Winston Churchill and President Roosevelt. In January 1943 they had met at Casablanca to decide the long-distant plans for the war, including the original blue-print for 'Overlord', the invasion of Europe, and the decision for the Americans to join in the bombing of Germany for which 'the primary object will be the progressive destruction and dislocation of the German military, industrial and economic system, and the undermining of the morale of the German people' (Casablanca directive).

In Europe meanwhile, Hitler continued to exert his strangling grip on the occupied countries, and threatened to annihilate his enemies with insuperable secret weapons.

On the Russian front, Stalin was beginning his offensive against the Germans, which during the summer was to signal great victories, particularly at Orel, Kharkov and Taganrog, which marked the ruin of the German army on the Eastern front.

We in Tunisia, however, were not to know of these future successes at the time of our arrival there. All we knew was that ever since El Alamein in October 1942, Field Marshal Rommel had steadily been on the retreat but was far from being defeated. His reputation as an almost super-human commander remained undiminished. His troops were now steadily dug in at Mareth in a line stretching from the sea to the steep Matmata mountains. Opposing him were the 50th, the 51st Highland Divisions and an Indian Division.

*Second World War, Vol V, p.6.

Before the main battle began, Rommel attacked with a formidable array of tanks. As the tanks moved forward they saw the British abandon their anti-tank defences and run away. But to their amazement they soon discovered that the defences were all dummies. When they gave chase they were shattered by the real anti-tank defences a short distance further on. Fifty-two German tanks were destroyed, with no British losses.

Montgomery then launched his main attack – a two pronged frontal assault by the 50th Division on the coast, and the New Zealand Division on a long left-hook mission round the Matmata mountains. Although the frontal attack was repulsed, the battle was finally won when the New Zealanders in an epic battle, through the German defences, allowing the 1st Armoured Division to make victory certain.

Meanwhile, in November 1942, the First Army with the 78th Division and the US Rangers made a surprise landing at Algiers. In spite of great difficulties of supply, they progressed along the coast as far as Medjez-el-Bab in Tunisia, meeting with only light opposition. There they were halted by the wet weather which bogged the supply route while the single track railway was bombed. The Germans meanwhile had reacted fast, first by sending Panzer troops under General von Arnim to seize Tunis and the important port of Bizerta, and to fortify the mountain, later known and Longstop, which formed a formidable defence bastion protecting Tunis.

This was basically the position when in early March 1943 the First Division, including the Guards Brigade and the Gordon Highlanders, landed at Algiers and rushed eastwards to the bleak hill country around Medjez-el-Bab. This was to be the scene of a series of desperately fierce and bloody battles against Germany's finest troops, until eventually the might of Rommel's Africa Korps was conquered and many thousands of troops were captured, complete with tanks, guns and equipment. In the cauldron of war that was to follow, we were, in January 1943, to become embroiled in the epic struggle on the Anzio beach-head. The landing at Anzio was devised by Winston Churchill to be the start of a diversion to withdraw German troops from the strongly held Monte Cassino, allow the Fifth Army to break through the German Gothic line, and with the British and American forces at Anzio to swarm northwards and capture Rome.

Instead, the Germans quickly sealed off the beach-head with an iron ring of tanks and devastating artillery fire. From the Alban hills the German guns sent down a continuous rain of shells onto every corner of the Allied positions, while the Panzer divisions thrust hard to drive us back into the sea.

All that took place fifty years ago; it is fitting now to remember all who were the victims of the horrors of war and who did not return.

PART I – TUNISIA

1
Operation Torch – to Tunis

The cold bleak mountain top in Tunisia was the last place one would want to spend the night. Yet here we were, with the prospect of enduring perhaps many days and nights. It was not only the incessant north-east wind that made life unpleasant, but the spasmodic shell-fire that came from the German artillery, exploding in and around our positions.

The mountain, known as the Djerbel Jaffa, was in fact not much higher than an arid and rocky hill, a mere dot on the map. Beneath it the Tunisian plain with the eerily sounding name of Goubellat, stretched to a dusty horizon, dominated by hills equally forbidding and made sinister by the presence of German troops.

Normally the Djerbel Jaffa was visited only by wandering wild goats, but now in March 1943, its slopes near the summit were pitted with slit-trenches and occupied by myself and thirty men, mainly from Aberdeen, comprising a platoon of B Company of the 6th Battalion, the Gordon Highlanders.

We had arrived on a moonless night after having left the staging camp near Bone on the tip of the North African coast. Then we had endured a sixteen hour road convoy over the mountains and through an endless barren wilderness, until we reached a deep valley. Here we formed up in companies and were led by guides to our first destination. My platoon was taken up a steep goat track to the top of the Djerbel Jaffa, ready to take over from a platoon of the East Surrey Regiment. Their officer greeted us warmly. In the dark I could hardly make out his features, but he seemed remarkably young. After showing us round the positions he gave me, as platoon commander, a few words of advice; 'Never show yourselves by day. The Germans spot any movement, so carry up water and rations by night only.'

'Where exactly are the enemy lines?' I asked.

'Just about all around,' he answered with a wide sweep of his arm. 'On those hills, and those, and those. There's no such thing as a line. It's just a case of who owns which hill.' He pointed down into the darkness, 'The enemy is very active all around Goubellat Plain – fighting patrols nearly every night – fifty or sixty strong. Beyond the valley to the north is Longstop Hill. The Jerries are sitting tight on top of it. They are the Hermann Goering Division – the best of all the German troops – blocking our way forward to Tunis.'

A soldier from the Surreys brought us each a mug of hot tea. 'Fifteen minutes to go, sir,' he announced. 'The platoon's all ready.' Soon they departed in single file down the goat track, dark shapes bearing heavy packs on their backs. We were alone in our bleak domain.

As the dawn brought a red flush behind the eastern hills, the wild panorama gradually revealed itself. Below us the Goubellat plain stretched for miles, lonely, apparently devoid of life, traversed by deep wadis and partly yellow with masses of African marigolds. Corn was growing too in uneven patches. But it was left to the winds with no one to harvest it.

Then as I looked back towards the north, I saw several flashes near the top of Longstop Hill. Some two seconds elapsed, then a vicious explosion shattered the hillside just below us. From a neighbouring hill about a mile away on which our C Company was established, came another crash followed by distant cries of 'Help, Help!' As they were too far away from us to aid them, we could only wait while the acrid smell of cordite drifted up to our positions. Then there was silence but for the wind. Perhaps the Germans were just carrying out their usual morning routine.

Later that morning a message came for me on the platoon's wireless set. 'Mr Grace to come down at once to the CO.' With some trepidation I hurried down the goat track to where Battalion HQ was established in a protected valley. The Commanding Officer, Lieut-Colonel James Peddie welcomed me with an encouraging smile. He was a tall man with a forceful personality, yet a lively sense of humour. His prominent chin and piercing eyes indicated his aggressive nature when it came to facing the enemy, and he expected his men to be equally dedicated.

'I have a job for you, Ted' he began without ado. 'The Brigadier is worried about the German patrols which seem to have the run of

Goubellat plain. You are to take three men tonight and make a full reconnaissance beyond Goubellat village to the group of farms.' He indicated a point on the map laid out on a collapsible table. 'Bring back as much information as you can, but don't let the Germans catch you. Be back before dawn. Good luck!'

So this was to be my first introduction to the war against Hitler. It was all so different to anything we had expected. Just myself and three men alone on a dark night on that desolate wilderness. Back on Djerbel Jaffa, I had to choose from the many volunteers to come with me. Then as it would be dark with only a quarter moon I had to memorise the entire route each way, both from the map and from what I could see of the plain.

The sun was setting in a golden scarlet as the four of us climbed down the slopes of Jaffa to wait in the foothills until dark. Then beneath a starry sky, we walked into the vast Goubellat Plain. I went first with pistol and compass, followed by Corporal Tripney, Parker and Christie. We were dressed in Commando fashion, with soft caps and ammunition in our pockets.

After about an hour walking through waist deep corn, we came to an open expanse where nothing grew but a mass of African marigolds. This made walking easier but more noisy, for the flowers knocked against our boots at every step. We stopped frequently in order to listen to the deep silence.

Suddenly I thought I heard a soft swishing noise coming from somewhere ahead. We dropped quietly to the ground. There could be no doubt about it; feet were approaching – evidently a large number of feet. We stretched ourselves flat on the ground, trying to look like marigolds. Against the rising moon we saw the black silhouettes of a large group of men coming directly towards us. The footsteps grew louder. There was nothing for it but to hold our breath and lie motionless.

They approached to within ten yards. I thought they must hear the loud beating of my heart. Then the patrol leader (perhaps after glancing at his compass) altered his course slightly to the left. They passed us at about five yards distance – more than fifty Germans complete with rifles and light machine guns, the complete fighting patrol. With my nose hidden behind a marigold I could see them perfectly and note all details for future reference. If only we had been a whole platoon instead of only four men we could have completely ambushed them. But it was not without intense relief that we saw them march on into the darkness.

Cautiously we stood up and continued marching on for a further hour. I began to think that we had missed our objective, the farms beyond the village of Goubellat. Then Corporal Tripney touched my arm. 'Look there, sir, is that a group of white buildings?'

'Perhaps you're right,' I agreed, peering through the darkness, 'twenty paces forward, then stop.'

We slowly approached the buildings which soon turned out to be a cluster of barns, with one larger stone building in the centre.

Suddenly we heard what must have been a clink of metal, as though digging was in progress, perhaps with spades on stony ground.

'Crawl forwards slowly,' I whispered. 'Parker watch out on the left, Christie on the right.'

From the cover of a nearby rock, we made out the shadowy figures of about a dozen Germans, working intently on the ground, about twenty yards in front of the nearest house.

'The bastards are laying mines!' I exclaimed in a husky whisper, 'ready for our next patrol.'

'Look sir,' muttered the sharp-eyed Tripney, 'there's a sentry standing all alone. He's got his back to us. I'm going to get him!'

'Too risky – the others will see you.'

'It's worth trying sir, I've always wanted to bag a sentry – ever since –'

I knew exactly what he meant. Some three months earlier, in what seemed to have been a different world, King George VI had come up to Scotland to inspect the troops and bid us farewell. With General Penney, the Divisional Commander and Colonel Peddie, he had watched a number of demonstrations, including my platoon's version of unarmed combat. Corporal Tripney had been the one to stalk a sentry, bring him down, tie up his mouth and drag him away, all in total silence.*

The King had seemed greatly amused by the demonstration. Could Tripney now succeed against a real German?

I hurriedly orderd the other two men to be ready to give covering fire if the mine-laying Germans reacted.

Tripney crawled forward. The sentry was still standing with his back to us. When Tripney had got to within ten yards he stood up and like a shadow eased himself forwards towards his victim. With a

---

*A photograph published in *The Scotsman* in 1943 shows King George VI watching this demonstration, including General Penney and the author (see plate section).

final bound, his right arm enfolded the German's throat, dragging him backwards towards us. We were ready with two knotted handkerchiefs. By the time he was released from Tripney's throttling grip, his mouth was firmly tied up. He tried to gasp, but no sound would come. We tied his wrists behind his back and pulled him away into the darkness, while Parker remained a few moments watching for any reaction from the mine-layers.

After some critical moments of dragging the German further away, we were safely out of earshot. Parker rejoined us. 'They're still digging, sir. We're OK.'

For nearly two hours we marched back towards the Djerbel Jaffa. At first the German who had been nearly choked by Tripney's arm could hardly stand. Prodded by Parker's rifle he stumbled on, grunting ineffectually beneath his gag. It was slow going, for we had frequently to stop and listen for enemy patrols, while I had to check the compass bearing.

Once we were alone in the wilderness we untied the German's gag. He was a burly, thick-set fellow, who surprised us by talking in English, evidently not at all dismayed at being captured. 'I speak English very goot,' he declared, 'since five years I am in England. I am unloading sheeps in Liverpool dock.'

'Get a move on', ordered Parker, jerking him forward with his rifle. 'No small talk here.'

'But now I go to England again, yes? Soon when Germany wins war, I go home. Better than fighting, yes?'

'You'll soon find out what's best for you! Keep your fucking mouth shut!'

After this polite conversation we pressed on in silence. In order to avoid the German patrol on its return, I decided to make a detour. We marched on past the marigolds until we had to cross a series of wadis. These normally were to be avoided owing to the chance of mines, booby traps or ambushes. Examining every step, I led the way down these deep clefts. Once at the bottom the effect was quite extraordinary. Tall cliffs of cracked sun-scorched clay seemed to tower above us like battlements seen in a fantastic dream. Black shadows were cast from the faint moonbeams to add to the weird silence and motionless black shapes.

Suddenly the night was shattered by a burst of machine gun fire, coming from about a mile away on our right. We could see tracer bullets flashing angrily at each other. Then followed a succession of bangs from mortars or grenades. The battle lasted about fifteen minutes, followed by complete silence. We learned next day that a platoon from one of our neighbouring units had returned from an uneventful patrol only to be ambushed by a large German patrol hiding at the very entrance to the British positions. The platoon commander was killed by the first burst of fire, and his sergeant wounded. The platoon went to ground and fought back hard. The enemy having achieved surprise began to disengage, taking with them one wounded prisoner. A few on both sides lay dead, but the Germans disappeared into the darkness, while stretcher bearers hurried down to rescue the wounded.

It was almost first light by the time we climbed up the steep slopes of the Djerbel Jaffa. We handed over our prisoner who still seemed pleased at the prospect of missing the rest of the war. I hurried down to report to Colonel Peddie. 'Good show Ted,' he said. 'Every prisoner helps, especially if he reveals the German dispositions. With our big attack coming soon –'

I looked at him in surprise. 'Yes, it's no secret,' he added, 'any day now the whole division will be moving on to drive the Germans out of Africa. Meanwhile you'll need a good sleep. You've had a long night.'

By the time the order to move on at last came, we had grown accustomed to the strange life on our mountain. In spite of the incessant wind, the occasional shelling from German artillery and several more uneventful patrols, we had adapted remarkably well. Now the prospect of being part of a major offensive against the formidable German divisions was, to say the least, daunting.

We knew that only a few weeks before, the Germans had inflicted heavy losses on the American II Corps down south at the Kesserine Pass. Now we were told the good news that the same US Corps under Generals Patton and Bradley had scored a notable victory at El Guettar. The German Fifth Panzer Army under General von Arnim had been badly mauled and was in retreat. The new commander of the British First Army in Tunisia was Field Marshal Alexander. Both the First and the Eighth Armies were to close on the Germans from the east and the south and drive them into the sea. The main objective was to be the capture of Tunis itself.

With this sparse knowledge, we formed up as soon as it was dark and followed in single file down the now familiar goat track to join the rest of the battalion in the valley. All night we marched to a new staging camp to prepare for the battle to come. At dawn we found ourselves in a deep wadi where poppies and thistles were flowering. Here we rested during the heat of the day. At nightfall we were given a good hot dinner and hoped for a peaceful few hours before marching on again.

Before midnight a runner from Major Bridgman, B Company Commander, woke us with an urgent message, 'Ten Platoon stand to! Full equipment. Mr. Grace to Major Bridgmen at once please.'

'Sorry to wake you Ted,' said the major, 'but the alarm bells are ringing. Enemy approaching. Take your platoon down the white track till you come to a hill with Wog huts. Stop the Jerries if you can. Good luck.'

Once more we were marching on down the track; it seemed just that sort of night when anything might happen. We found the little hill on which were scattered Arab hovels. Suddenly the darkness was stabbed by a brilliant flash coming from the low ground in front. This turned into a mass of flames, punctuated by hundreds of minor explosions and splashes of fire – apparently from an ammunition lorry burning. A machine gun opened up from a hill on the right, with tracer bullets searching the darkness.

Immediately I put my three sections into position on the slope of our hill. Then another fiery explosion came, much nearer. A German patrol was evidently approaching, firing lorries on the way. Tracer bullet flashed over our heads. We had no cover but the darkness. No one moved but I knew that an anxious finger was on every trigger.

Then we could see a long line of black figures approaching through the darkness, until the whole slope below us seemed to be crowded with dark shapes, quickly growing larger.

Every man in my platoon seemed to have frozen into the earth. I waited a few more seconds that seemed endless, until each German presented an accurate target, and then heard my voice shouting 'Fire!'

At the first volley from our two forward sections, the enemy sank to the ground. We could see nothing. I had no idea how many had been hit. After a few moments silence their mortar opened up. Several bombs burst just in front of us, while their machine gun fire tore the air over our heads. It was high time for us to move to new positions. I shouted for all to crawl backwards. Every man glided silently backwards, without raising an inch from the ground. Then at a new line about twenty yards back we stopped, waiting.

A fresh burst of enemy fire came from a ridge on our right. In case they charged down on us from the higher ground, I swung two sections round to meet the challenge. More mortar bombs burst in the very positions we had just left, followed by another explosion further down the hill. Then another further away. 'They must be withdrawing and firing more trucks on the way.' In case they returned I reorganised the platoon, and then went round to see if we had suffered casualties. Two men were slightly hurt, but one dark shape lay motionless. It was Private Parker, dead with a bullet through his throat. I felt an ache in my stomach. The Germans had gone but we had lost one of our finest soldiers. Parker had been with me on the first patrol across Goubellat Plain.

I sent Reay, my batman, back to report to Major Bridgman. While we waited I took three men with me to reconnoitre the surrounding area. In the distance the gutted lorries were still smouldering and sending out sparks and flashes. A peculiar sound came from one of the nearby huts. In the smelly darkness inside we found that the hovel was being used as a makeshift first aid post. Several men were lying on dirty straw, while a soldier tried to make them comfortable.

'We're truck drivers, sir' explained the man, 'part of B Eschelon. We were taken by surprise as we were unloading our vehicles. We got no warning – they set our trucks alight and took us prisoner.'

How many casualties?'

'We've got five here. Three of our chaps. They're not too bad. And two Jerries, they're pretty bad, sir.'

'Did you bring them all in here?' I asked.

'Oh no sir, it was the Germans brought us all in, both their wounded and ours. One of their men must have been a stretcher bearer for he dressed all the wounds and patched them up. Then there was another who could speak English a bit. He gave us cigarettes and told me to stay behind and look after them. Then they all went off taking two of our chaps prisoner.'

I reassured him that an ambulance would be sent as quickly as possible and returned to the rest of the platoon.

At last came the early signs of dawn, and with it we saw Major Bridgman and the other two platoons of B Company. Behind them came A Company who passed through our positions and on to find the enemy. By daylight we saw great activity on the wide plain stretching around Grenadier Hill. A squadron of Churchill tanks opened fire onto some unseen target in the distance.

I suddenly felt a wave of weariness overtake me. We had long been without sleep, and the surroundings became unreal. Our brief skirmish was over, but we knew that this had been nothing but a prelude. The real offensive was about to begin.

2
The Attack

The evening before our offensive, the whole of the First British Division was assembled in a long valley with the range of hills known as Banana Ridge casting deep shadows. Above us the German Hermann Goering Division with tanks and artillery waited in strength, a formidable army, well equipped and determined to fight for every yard.

As soon as it was dark, we had to march ten miles to the start-line. Then a massive artillery box-barrage would pulverise the enemy positions, while we infantry would form up, fix bayonets and follow the exploding shells until we reached the German trenches on the hill top.

As the background to battle, the elements created a Wagnerian setting; black thunder clouds massed in the south, slowly overwhelming the white cumulus which hovered over the hills aflame with the scarlet of the setting sun. The rumble of thunder mingled with distant gunfire, and flashes of lightning threw the cloud formations into stark relief. Soon the rain began to fall, while a brilliant rainbow spanned the mountains – an emblem of peace contrasting with the fulminations of war.

The turbulence of the atmosphere emphasised the intense feeling of foreboding that gripped our minds during the anxious period of waiting. Thoughts of home took on a new meaning. Life itself was something quite wonderful; our future years – if only we might live to enjoy them – offered the most exciting prospects.

So the last few hours of preparation passed. After we had been given a hot dinner, the Commanding Officer walked around with encouraging words, rather like Henry V before Agincourt. We were all outwardly cheerful, making jokes and pretending the night was for adventure.

Then came the time to fall in. After fixing our equipment with its heavy weight of ammunition and grenades, rations for twenty-four hours, and the few necessaries which would be our entire luggage for days or perhaps weeks, we assembled in order of platoons.

THE BATTLES OF BANANA RIDGE, LONGSTOP AND BOU AOUKAZ
APRIL/MAY 1943

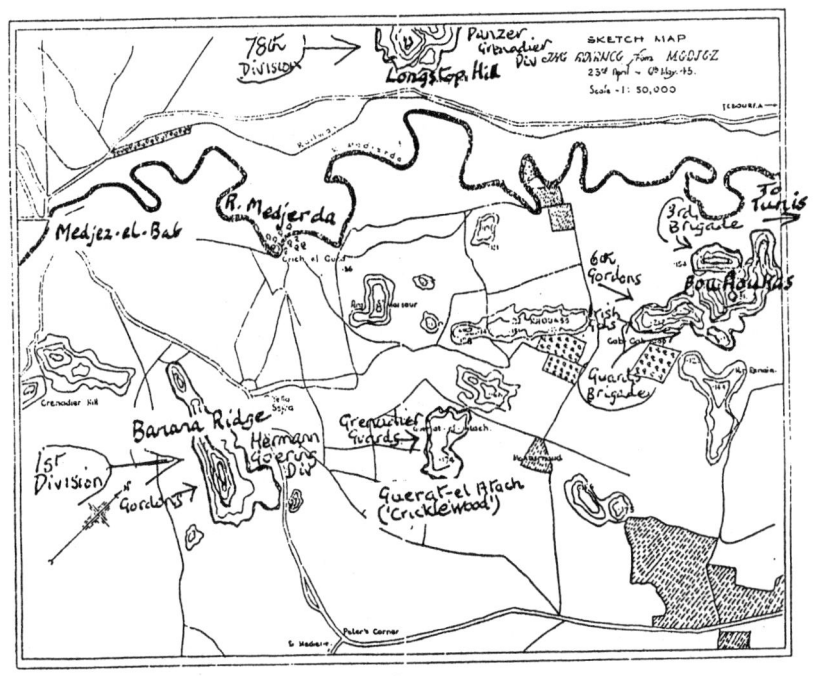

It was quite dark as we marched off, the rain falling steadily and the thunder rumbling like an angry giant as it slowly moved away. Colonel Peddie led the way as we tramped along a rough and stony track. My platoon was next in the order of march. No one spoke except for an occasional mutter as someone tripped on a boulder. After an hour the rain stopped and the half moon rose behind a bank of clouds. The track led onto a road which was crowded with tanks, lorries and guns, ambling slowly into position. As we came up to them in the darkness, these great lumbering monsters assumed outlandish shapes, looming over us like nightmarish ogres.

Soon we crossed the road and moved into a dark mountain pass which led us upwards until we came to the main Medjes-Tunis road. This was to be the forming-up line. Guides from the Intelligence section were waiting for us and led us to the white tapes which marked the start line.

In five minutes we were to start the attack.

The rest of the night was like a fantastic dream. Exactly on zero hour we started to move forward. The moon was now shining in a clear sky, and we could see the hill we were to capture. All the fatigue from the long march had vanished and even the heavy load on our backs seemed to have been lifted.

Then, as expected, the artillery barrage opened with a shattering roar. It was exactly 2.28am. Shells screamed just over our heads with savage ferocity, exploding on the hillside above us in hellish fury. It was essential for us to advance steadily up the hill, keeping as close to the bursts of our own shells as possible, so that when the barrage lifted we would be right on top of the enemy positions.

Suddenly the moonlight was obscured and we found ourselves engulfed in thick clouds of smoke, while the acrid tang of cordite fumes filled our throats. This was the extra cover of a smoke screen laid down by the artillery by way of additional protection, as well as the prodigious pounding by the HE shells. The whole mountain was now transformed into an inferno. We could see only a few yards in front of us, but stumbled on following the compass bearing. The creeping barrage was to move forwards a hundred yards every two minutes. Whatever happened we had to keep up with it. The tremendous noise and smoke seemed as though we were in the very midst of the exploding shells, and indeed one or two did land just behind us.

Suddenly the thunder of the shells ceased; for a few moments there was an eerie silence until we heard the sputter of machine guns somewhere over on the left. (The Loyals had found themselves almost on top of a nest of enemy machine guns. Lieut Sandys Clerk had crawled forwards alone towards the guns and thrown grenades until one after another he destroyed every gun. For this and other exploits he was later awarded the VC.)

As the smoke blew away, we saw that we were almost on top of the mountain. On our sector there was still no sign of the enemy. We reached a series of slit trenches, all totally abandoned. Major Bridgman hurriedly overtook us.

'Find forward defensive positions fast!' he ordered. 'The Germans must have avoided the shelling, now they will attack us.'

This as we we were to learn was a favourite trick of the Germans when they knew an attack was imminent: withdraw, avoid casualties, then hit hard, catching us (they hoped) on the wrong foot.

It was then 5.15 and already the first light was beginning to appear. I could make out the lie of the sloping ground in front of us, so leading my platoon at the double, I found a favourable site where we could command a good field of fire facing the area probably occupied by the Germans.

'Dig fast!' I shouted. 'They'll be on us any moment!'

Even as I spoke the first mortar bombs landed near us.

With only small entrenching tools it was impossible to dig fast enough, yet every man plied into the stony ground, realising that his very life depended on his efforts. More bombs landed in our midst while the only shelter we had was shallow scratchings a few inches deep.

Then in the swish and thunder of the explosions came the agonised cry of a wounded man. The shout went up 'Stretcher Bearer!' For about half an hour the mortar barrage continued. More cries came from wounded men. In spite of the intense danger the stretcher bearers ran in, lifted the casualties and carried them off. How it was that they somehow dodged the mortars seemed a miracle.

The firing stopped suddenly. In the ensuing silence we saw a long line of grey figures moving towards us over the skyline. On they came walking in a long line through waist high corn. Then behind them another line in fan-like order, all carrying rifles or Spandau machine guns. 'Keep down!' I called to my platoon. 'Don't fire 'til I shout!'

Evidently the Germans were unaware of our positions, for at first they made no attempt to attack. As though to draw our fire the men in the first wave shouted 'Hello Tommy! Tipperary! Wakey Wakey!'

I waited a few more moments until the oncoming Germans presented a perfect target. 'Fire!' I yelled.

With our first volley of Bren, rifle and mortar fire every single German sank to the ground, disappearing into the thick corn. Shouts came which sounded like fire orders mingled with cries for help. As the corn reached right up to the edge of our positions, they might crawl to within a few yards of us without being seen. In order to forestall this danger, I decided to take my platoon round to one side to attack them first. So waving to the men, now reduced to about twenty-five, we crawled to a slight rise in the ground in the hope of seeing where the enemy were hiding. More shouts came from various directions, indicating that they had spread out over a wide area.

A sudden ping sounded as a bullet hit a corn ear just by my head.

'Sounds as though they're trying to surround us, sir' whispered Corporal Boyes, kneeling beside me. 'I don't see which way we're going to attack them.'

'Neither do I yet' I admitted. 'There must be hundreds of them hidden in the corn.

We crawled on further until rapid bursts of Spandau fire came from several different directions. Harsh guttural voices optimistically shouted 'Hands Up! Hands Up!'

With no visible targets, it would have been useless to waste ammunition, so we made a dash to a small hillock partly hidden behind stunted trees. Another voice shouted in my ear, 'Hello Grace, what the hell are you crawling about here for?' Peering through the corn stalks, I found myself almost on top of Major Sinclair, the commander of the Gunner Battery. 'If you're looking for anything,' he went on, 'you've just discovered my OP.'

'We're trying to attack those Jerries,' I answered, 'if only I knew exactly where they are.'

'What Jerries?'

'Those all around us in the corn, of course.'

'Those aren't Jerries, they're our own men. Didn't you hear them shouting at us?'

My exasperation at this reply was interrupted by more shouts from a remarkably near-at-hand German and a burst of bullets just over our heads. Major Sinclair was convinced. Grabbing the hand-set of his portable telephone, he gave hurried orders to his gunners. To me he added, 'We'll fix 'em! Get your platoon back behind our line of fire and watch the fireworks.'

A few moments later we had run back to our original fox holes – or rather, scratchings in the ground. At this moment the Germans began their attack. Rising from their hiding places in the corn at a strident shout of command, they ran towards us firing their rifles wildly. Again our platoon let off a burst from every weapon. Many of the Germans fell but many more were to follow. Before they could get on top of us a violent shriek of shells screamed overhead and explosions burst in their midst. Major Sinclair's fireworks had started just in time! Some of the Germans fell, others kept on charging towards us only to run into the accurate Bren gun and rifle fire from our platoon.

Shells continue to rain down onto the corn. The Germans who were in the second wave ran back, some falling, others getting away like rabbits in a hayfield.

As soon as the attack seemed to be over, I hurried to see how we had suffered. Two men were dead; three more with superficial injuries from flying bullets. While we helped to apply field dressings to their wounds, sounds of fierce fighting came from both the left and right of us. As we had had no time to consolidate our positions, we had no means of knowing what was happening to the companies nearby. Apart from Major Sinclair it seemed as though we were alone and isolated on this bleak, exposed hilltop.

The most urgent task for us was to enlarge the very inadequate holes that were supposed to be slit trenches. But within a few moments a new and violent shelling from German artillery started. We must have been within full view of the enemy, for mortar bombs and shells landed accurately in our midst. Then a new threat was added; on the next ridge only about half a mile distant, a German Tiger tank lumbered over the skyline and was firing an 88mm gun at us with shattering effect. We could do nothing but squeeze our bodies as far as possible into our shallow holes and pray.

All that morning the pounding went on. Every few seconds the earth shook. A continual shower of stones and soil and bits of shrapnel pattered down on us. I watched the shallow walls of my trench gradually crumbling from the continual blast, and wondered how it was that nothing had hit me. I remember reflecting that this was Good Friday, and that at home this would be a holiday; soon the church bells would be ringing for Easter. But now there was nothing but the mad scream of the shells and the head-splitting crash of the explosions.

There was turbulence everywhere. The earth was in convulsions as our own artillery kept up a continuous barrage over a wide area. This no doubt prevented the enemy from mounting a further attack across the open ground in front of us.

To our tremendous relief, a shell scored a direct hit on the Tiger tank that was strafing us. The gun was put out of action and the tank's tracks were blown off rendering it immobile. Now was our chance to move. I jumped up, amazed to be alive. We had suffered many casualties. Several men had received direct hits and were no more, apart from steel helmets and one or two boots lying as obscene memorials. Other men were wounded needing urgent attention. I sent a runner to try to find stretcher bearers. Even now there was a risk of stray shells landing near us, but we few remaining unscathed could achieve nothing but try to help the wounded. One man who had lost his leg from the knee was carried away by two other men. Eight of us who were unhurt stayed to look after ten men who had sustained various wounds. The wait seemed endless, but in what must have been only a few minutes, two pairs of stretcher bearers arrived at the double.

After that I have only the vaguest recollection of how we all got away from that benighted exposed hilltop. I remember helping an injured man to the Regimental Aid Post. Here the doctor was working hard with a line of waiting casualties. A mug of strong very sweet tea was put into my hand. In all my life I doubt if any cup of tea was more welcome or more restorative, although my hand was shaking and I spilt a few drops. Strangely, although deeply saddened by the loss of good men, I felt unaccountably happy. It was indeed good to be alive!

3
Minefields and Tanks

After making sure all the wounded were being looked after in the Regimental Aid Post, I was able to move into a cornfield sheltered by a rocky outcrop and assemble the few remaining members of my platoon. Fortunately Sergeant Maclaren was one of the few to have returned unscathed. He had proved himself to be entirely dependable, always in command of any situation, and was respected by all the men. Aged about thirty, he was tall, carrying himself with military precision. Corporals Tripney and Boyes had both received cuts and gashes to the face from flying splinters of rock, while the two indomitable Bren gunners Craig and Watson had flesh wounds from German bullets, but were both cheerful and, like all of us, happy to be alive. They had fearlessly exposed their heads while blazing off their weapons at the attacking Germans, and with the platoon's rapid rifle fire had been largely instrumental in repelling the enemy.

As the immediate danger had subsided, we had at last the chance to open our haversacks and make a late afternoon breakfast of the inevitable bully beef and hard tack biscuits (which at that time were as good as any banquet at the Ritz). Even now our mouthfuls were punctuated with odd shells bursting nearby, while a few German snipers who had been left behind in the corn would fire at any figure rash enough to stand up as an easy target.

The warm sunshine and the dust from the cornfield made my eyes heavy with drowsiness, but it was essential for me to find Major Bridgman. He had established a temporary Company HQ behind some rocks, and was busy writing out casualty lists.

After greeting me, he said, 'It seems you have only ten men left, Ted?'

'That's right. It was that blasted Tiger tank that did most of the damage. The ground was so rocky we couldn't dig in properly. You can guess what it was like. How are the other platoons?'

'They had a pasting, but not so badly as you. The ground was evidently not so rocky and they managed to dig proper holes before the attack began.'

'I'm just so sorry we lost so many good men.'

Major Bridgman did not reply at first. He was a father figure to his company, and had every man's welfare at heart. 'Yes,' he said at length, 'we shall have a lot of letters to write to grieving relatives.'

He then moved over to his map case. 'You'll see here how the Battalion is disposed at this moment. As you know. A Company are on our right. According to the latest messages, they've reached their objective and are sitting tight. Tonight C Company in reserve will move through their positions and mop up any enemy pockets. Likewise D Company will move on in front of us, so you and your ten good men can dig yourselves cosy fox holes for tonight – but don't forget to post sentries. We've been promised a hot dinner after dark – so good appetite!'

I returned to my depleted platoon's position in the corn where the men were busy digging new slit trenches. 'Come and join us, sir' invited Sergeant Maclaren. 'We'll soon build a happy home. Any sign of grub?'

'Hot dinner after dark. D Company are coming through, so we'll be out of the firing line for tonight.'

The men gave a cheer. Reay, my batman, had already dug a trench about a foot deep. With his massive shoulders he made short work of the excavation. He was a fierce fighter and a crack shot with a rifle. The other few men still remaining were all young in their early twenties, coming mainly from Aberdeen or Peterhead, although one, Laurence Mingo, had until recently been a textile inspector in Toronto and was a keen ice hockey player.

By the time that we had queued for hot stew and duff, we were well organised. Seldom had a meal tasted so good. We seemed to be surrounded by a strange aura of happiness mingled with sadness for the loss of friends and a dull dread for what was to come.

Sleep was our most urgent need. Even down a stony fox hole I fell into a deep dreamless sleep. During the night D Company moved on beyond our positions removing any remaining pockets of the enemy. At the same time C Company, commanded by Major Forbes, swept clear the forward slopes beyond A Company. Lieut (later Major) Leslie Hatt described the scene:

'We crossed a deep ditch, which proved a real obstacle to the heavy laden. I could see the enemy's white tracer slowly loping towards us, then our red tracer flashing back in reply. We reformed and carried on in double time. Soon I found that my platoon were detached from the battle as there was no sign of the rest of the Company. Eventually I met CSM Murphy and Major Forbes, the Company commander. A short council of war was held and we miraculously discovered that we were on our objective. Our Company carrier arrived with tools and ammunition. Lieut Robin Bain, the carrier officer, did a magnificent job in locating us in the dark through the minefields. My first sight in the dawn was Lieut Bobby Smith dashing through our positions, a bandage round his head and a pistol at the ready. All rather like something out of a 1914 war picture. That morning the Germans gave us mortars and artillery shells of all types and even the personal attention of Stukas. It was a busy day. A Company did a magnificent job of work. They received infantry and tank counter-attacks in addition to other novelties.'

With only ten men, my platoon was no longer a fighting force. Yet there was much we could do. Before dawn that morning we heard the noises of battle. 'Sounds as though A Company are getting a pasting!' remarked Sergeant Maclaren. As he spoke a heavy artillery bombardment shattered the far side of Banana Ridge. The Germans were clearly renewing their attack all along the front. All that day A Company stood firm under heavy fire, repelling constant attacks. Thanks to the inspiring leadership of Major Robert Rae the Company yielded not an inch in spite of mounting casualties.

With my ten men I moved up to A Company positions and helped to escort the wounded men back to the Regimental Aid Post. During the morning occasional strafing Messerschmits paid us some attention, but only succeeded in providing good sport for our Bren gunners, Craig and Watson. It was a grand sight to watch those two grimy and dust-covered warriors blazing away at the German planes. We gave great cheers as we saw flames and black smoke coming from the tail of a Messerschmidt as it had zoomed over our heads.

All day the sun blazed down upon us and scorched our faces. We longed for sleep but the shell-fire and the constant need to keep alert was paramount. Thirst was now a growing problem. Our waterbottles were empty, but neither the water carts nor ration lorries could pass up the narrow track until darkness hid them from the German artillery. That night I took three men on a patrol down into the valley beyond the ridge. It was an eerie experience as we had to keep in the shadows and listen to the faint mutterings of German voices on the opposite hill. At least I was able to report back with some information as to the enemy positions.

Away on our left the sounds of a fierce battle continued. The North Staffords and the Loyals were enduring a tremendous barrage of fire, as the Hermann Goering Division threw every man and every weapon into a concentrated effort to recapture the ridge of hills. As the casualties mounted the Brigadier decided to withdraw the two battalions. A unit of the Fourth Division was sent to fill the gap and drive back the enemy. But the Germans were as solid in defence as aggressive in attack. The unit was forced to withdraw, leaving it to the artillery to launch an intense barrage to stabilise the position.

For two days the battle seemed to have reached a stalemate, both sides exhausted and licking their wounds. On the second morning just before dawn, I received an urgent message to see Major Bridgman. He was looking tired and worried. In a grim voice he said, 'Stanley Martin is lying out in a minefield – foot blown off. Stretcher bearers are already on the way. Take your men and help to bring him back.' He gave me a map reference. 'He was on patrol across that slope. Watch out for snipers and more mines.'

Within a few moments I had assembled the men and in the growing light of dawn hurried to the slope where Murray and Gordon, at great risk to their own lives, had already carried the injured man away from the minefield. Stanley Martin, the officer of 12 platoon, was a good friend to us all. Small of stature but big-hearted, he had a lively and kind disposition, seldom without a smile and a joke. But now on the stretcher he was clearly dazed, the pain showing in his face as the initial shock wore off. We managed to get him back to the Regimental Aid Post without further incident, and left him in the good hands of Doc, Captain G McIntosh, who had treated and evacuated most of the previous day's casualties.

Major Bridgman was also there to give Stanley words of encouragement. We felt very bitter about this incident. A hidden minefield always seemed to be a sinister and horrible menace to foot soldiers, especially during the hours of darkness. Death and injury lay waiting beneath the earth, silent and cowardly, for one could never fight back against them, or even know of their evil presence.

Earlier that same night two men of the 4th Division had been trapped in a minefield. Colonel Peddie had received urgent calls for help as his HQ was nearby. Captain McIntosh, always at the ready, with Lieut Robin Bain set out with stretcher bearers on a rescue mission. Unfortunately the mines could not be seen in the dark.

Another mine exploded injuring four of the rescue party including Doc McIntosh. (We had not realised when he was attending to Stanley Martin that he had been hurt in the leg and was carrying on regardless.) Before the party got away, a third mine went off injuring McPherson, one of the stretcher bearers. He was carried back but sadly died later of his wounds.

Mines were of course an essential part of any army's defence system. It was ironic that it fell to me on the third night to take my few men, first to reconnoitre a suitable harbour for tanks and then to stand on guard while the sappers laid a minefield to protect them. This was the initial stage of a plan to break the deadlock and attack on a wide front. As I had already explored the valley on the previous patrol, I had a fair idea of possible sites. We found a fold in the hillside where the tanks could assemble. Within a few hours I had reported back and a squadron of Churchills moved very slowly into position, keeping the sound of their engines to the minimum. Only a few hours of darkness remained for the mines to be laid. It was a strange and weird experience standing guard while silent figures moved up the track carrying the mines, while others with white tapes marked out and plotted the field. Quickly the sappers went on their knees planting and arming the mines. The night was silent but for occasional distant shell-fire and a strange wailing clank, the sound of which I shall never forget. It came from the iron sails of a wind pump that was pointing up into the dark sky like a gaunt giant with flailing arms. The night was made more horrible by the wind which not only sounded the eerie wail, but brought the smell of death from the scene of recent battles.

At last the long night came to an end. We all realised that a new offensive must begin soon – unless the Germans got in first with the massive troops and tanks at their disposal. Yet for three more days we remained in these positions in the cornfield. Nearly all day long the whine of shells passed over our heads as the enemy artillery pounded the only road for bringing up our supplies. We could see the shells landing almost beside the slow lumbering lorries. Yet in spite of one of two direct hits, the vehicles continued to move onwards imperturbably. Not surprisingly, our rations did not always arrive and our water supply was limited to one water-bottle a day for all purposes. Soon we became dust-caked, unshaven and sunburnt. One morning, however, some letters arrived from home, including for me a leaflet including Spencer's 'Prothalamium'. Instead of the noisy bullet and shell-shattering heat, I could read that somewhere –

> Calm was the day, and through the trembling air
> sweet breathing Zephyrus did softly play –
> A gentle spirit that lightly did delay
> Hot Titan's beams, which then did glisten fair . . .
> Sweet Thames run softly till I end my song!

This in turn reminded me of Rabbie Burns:

> Flow gently, sweet Afton, among thy green braes,
> Flow gently, I'll sing thee a song in thy praise.
> My Mary's asleep by thy murmuring stream,
> Flow gently, sweet Afton, disturb not her dream.

Soon after midnight, reinforcements arrived to make our platoon up to full strength. We were very relieved to be an effective force again, but it was hard for the newcomers from Scotland to adjust to these strange surroundings. Compared with us hardened warriors, they looked so pale-faced and innocent! We tried to welcome them and put them at their ease – not an easy matter when all we could offer them was the prospect of a major attack against heavily defended positions.

The present situation was explained to us at a briefing of the company and platoon commanders by Colonel Peddie. Compared with us he was looking remarkably spruce and clean-shaven, yet grimly determined. 'Now that the battalion is up to strength again,' he began, 'we can expect a major part in our coming offensive. If you look at the map here, you'll see that the Germans have two prominent hills which they have strongly fortified – Djerbel Ammera, known as Longstop Hill, and Bou Aoukas. Both of them guard the wide valley of the Medjerda River, which provides the direct route to Tunis. Therefore it is essential to capture these two features before the whole German army can be annihilated. 78 Division has already begun the assault on Longstop, and we shall follow next to take the Bou. That's all I can tell you at the moment. First of course we have to eliminate all the remaining enemy in our area. As soon as I receive more detailed orders I shall let you know. Thank you gentlemen.'

We returned to our platoons somewhat dazed by the prospect of the tremendous task that lay ahead. The whole outcome of the war might depend on the ultimate victory in North Africa, where so many decisive battles had already been fought. For Hitler the prospect of a humiliating defeat for his renowned Afrika Korps must have been appalling, while for Churchill and the Allies it was essential to clear the enemy from this continent before planning the invasion of Europe.

4
The Awesome Bou Aoukaz

To the north of the river Medjerda rose the massive bulk of Longstop Hill. Over nine hundred feet high, it dominated the terrain, casting a forbidding shadow over the valley. Partly covered with deep green whins, it looked a sinister bastion frowning over the plains bright with corn and poppies. For months the Germans had built what they thought to be impregnable defences into the very heart of the mountain, with trenches deep below the surface, and bunkers containing large supplies of food, water and ammunition. The guns were able to fire from under an iron-plated shield, while the approaches were defended by extensive minefields. This, with the Bou Aoukaz, formed the twin fortresses protecting the western approaches to Tunis from the Allies.

For many weeks the 78th Division had been fighting their way along the approaches to Longstop. A captured officer of the Panzer Grenadiers assured them that the mountain was impregnable. Yet however formidable the task, the main assault began at the end of April. First an intense creeping artillery barrage pounded the lower slopes and pulverised the hillside until it had exploded at least some of the minefields and rained shells on the German positions. Then behind the barrage stormed the Royal West Kents and the Argylls. Disaster struck from the start. Many men ran onto mines which the barrage had not destroyed. From the top of the mountain intense machine gun fire rained down upon them. They withdrew until dawn when they attacked again after a further artillery barrage. This time the West Kents, the Surreys and the Argylls made a concerted attempt to reach the summit, and with the support of tanks firing from a hill opposite, managed to secure a foothold on a prominent spur. The terrible day came to an end after many wounded men had been carried away in trucks and Bren-carriers to waiting ambulances. All night long the battle continued while the hill became an inferno, with machine guns, mortars and artillery clashing with each other and raining death and injury to both sides. At the end of three days and nights the repeated attacks and continual bombardment at last overcame the German resistance.

The final irresistible series of charges had been inspired by Major Anderson of the Argylls. After their Commanding Officer had been killed, the major took over the battalion and led a night attack up the final slope. Running through minefields and defying the stream of bullets, he led his men straight into the enemy. Many fell but others followed him from one hilltop to another, charging with bayonets, hurling grenades and yelling with fury as they shattered the terrified defenders. The momentum took them to the top of the hill when a Verey light pierced the night sky, signalling that Longstop had at last been captured. Major Anderson was later awarded the VC.

The final fortress standing guard against our advance was the Djerbel Bou Aoukaz. The next day the First Division was ordered to begin the offensive. The 800ft high mountain was, if anything, even more difficult to attack than Longstop. Its rocky sides were precipitous and the main feature was protected by machine guns on two hills on either side which gave cross-fire covering every yard of ground.

General Penney gave the Guards Brigade the privilege of launching the main assault. The Grenadiers had already captured the nearby village of Crich el Oued (soon christened 'Cricklewood'), and on 27 April the three Guards Battalions were ordered to attack the Bou. Following them, the Gordons were to follow through and consolidate.

We set off in high hopes that this would be the final major battle leading to the total surrender of all the German forces in North Africa. After a long night march we reached a wide plain covered with cornfields and poppies. A, B and D Companies were dispersed and hidden in the deep corn. As the night faded and in the early flush of dawn, the prospect in front of us was awe-inspiring. The great mass of the Bou Aoukaz towered over us like a threatening monster. No enemy could be seen but we knew that they were ready with immense fire-power in strongly fortified positions.

All day we waited, dozing in the heat, too thirsty to want to eat our dry rations. The plains were ominously silent but for the wind shimmering in the corn-stalks.

Then at four o'clock in the afternoon, one platoon of the Irish Guards moved off a quarter of an hour in advance of the rest of the company in order to secure the battalion startline. As they began to cross half a mile of open ground, the Germans opened fire. We watched appalled as the ground exploded with shell fire and machine guns which mercilessly swept a hail of lead into the defenceless Irish. It seemed that most of them must have been killed in the first few minutes, but behind them rushed the remaining companies of the Guards.

As darkness mercifully obscured their advance, we listened with trepidation as the sounds of the fiercest battle continued. We watched the yellow tracer bullets chasing each other up the mountain side, to be met by the flying horror of bullets and shells on the attackers. Then at last at one in the morning, the time came for us to move forward. A Company under Major Rae and D Company under Major Fleming led the way beyond the corn to the lower slopes. I followed next with my platoon, two-thirds of which were new arrivals, about to experience their first baptism of fire. Then came Major Bridgman and the other two platoons of B Company.

The acrid smell of cordite drifted down to us as the whole mountain seemed to be erupting. As we climbed higher we came within the fury of the battle. No longer able to see the company in front of us, we seemed to be engulfed in chaos. All we could do was struggle upwards, tripping over rocks and clefts, deafened by the din of explosions and machine guns. I called to the men to close up; on no account must the newcomers think they were lost. (The fact that I felt lost was a different matter.)

Then two wounded Irish Guardsmen helping each other stumbled downwards towards us. 'It's utter Hell up there!' one exclaimed. 'Dead bodies everywhere!'

This did little to encourage us. A shell exploded very near, knocking the breath from our lungs. A sudden wind swept down on us, laden with gunpowder fumes. Above all this, a strident voice, probably that of Major Rae, pierced the cacophany, 'Once more men, Charge!' Then followed a tremendous outburst of firing from every weapon, clashing with German machine guns.

I decided to avoid this part of the battle or we might find ourselves firing on our own men. Instead we climbed a slope to the right which seemed to lead to the summit. A burst of Spandau fire in front of us showed that we were almost on the enemy trenches. In the ensuing confusion I lost all sense of time or reality. I remember we all fired in a scrambling fury while a spray of bullets passed over and among us. How it happened I cannot tell, but somehow we reached the hilltop and jumped into the German slit-trenches. Where were the Germans now? Some lay dead around us, but the remainder must have retreated down the reverse slopes, no doubt to regroup and prepare to counter-attack.

With Sergeant Maclaren I hurriedly checked our platoon. Sadly two men were mising; we found them lying dead further down the hillside. Corporals Boyes and Tripney had bullet wounds but were temporarily patched up. Reay, my batman, had a nasty leg wound and with another man needed urgent attention. The sounds of battle had now died down. In the starlight we soon made contact with Major Bridgman and the rest of the Company, precariously established on a spur of the hill nearby. The attack had, it seemed, been successful and A and D Companies were now relieving the battered Guards.

Our urgent task, once the two injured men had been carried down the hill, was to prepare for the inevitable counter-attack. The German trenches which we now occupied were of course facing the wrong way, so I warned the men that when the enemy began their attack we would have to crawl forwards to the edge of a long ledge of rock to fire down on them.

The remaining hours of the night were bitterly cold, an added hazard for those who had lost blood with various wounds. At five o'clock, shortly before sunrise, a shattering series of explosions pounded our mountain top. Sheltering deep in the newly acquired trenches we were relatively safe from these, until new diabolical missiles – so called butterfly bombs, burst overhead, showering lethal shrapnel down on top of us. One sudden crash jarred my head; a jagged piece of metal had struck my steel helmet, denting but mercifully not piercing it. Several men were not so lucky. Sergeant Maclaren was struck in the back by a piece of shrapnel. Once again the call for stretcher bearers resounded. Braving all the hazards these men rushed to the rescue and carried the wounded men away from the exposed ridge. Lance Corporal Allardice was now the only uninjured NCO. I shouted to him to take over as platoon sergeant.

After half an hour the bombardment ceased. In the sudden silence I gave the order to crawl forward. We reached a commanding position overlooking the slopes below. As expected German infantry were climbing up towards us. We waited until they were near enough to present easy targets, then with a blaze of fire from all weapons we sent them reeling backwards. More were to follow. They now knew exactly where we were, so we received a barrage of fire from rifles and mortars, some splintering on the rocks but most flying harmlessly overhead. The vicious exchange continued, the Germans sheltering behind rocks and broken ground.

Major Bridgman suddenly ran up the slope behind us. 'The Jerries have gained a foothold along the ridge on your right,' he exclaimed. 'You'll have to drive them off. 11 and 12 Platoons will give concentrated fire for two minutes. Then go in. Zero in five minutes from now. Good luck!'

He ran back to order the fire from the other platoons. I had four minutes left to organise the attack. In spite of his bleeding arm, Corporal Boyes called to me, 'I'm with you, sir, I'm OK.' 'Me too!' shouted Corporal Tripney.

'Well done!' I called back, 'Corporal Boyes and I will go first, Tripney and Moir fire all the way. Allardice organise the mortar fire and pick off any Jerries who try to run for it.'

No amount of army training could have prepared us for this. The ridge was so narrow that the normal formation of alternating sections attacking with covering fire from the others was impossible. Fortunately time did not give us the chance to think of the risks. It was a game; those who came in first would survive but there would be no also-rans. Every man ran the race with death or a free ride with the stretcher bearers.

Four minutes passed. Then our two platoons opened up with intensive fire power. Two more minutes of devastating explosions and flying bullets. We waited tensely. Then silence. We left the ledge of rocks and ran with bayonets fixed along the narrow goat track to where the enemy waited. We fired and yelled defiance as we ran. The combined effect of fire power and our charge seemed too much for the enemy. One or two put up their hands, the others ran headlong down the long hillside. Once again we found ourselves in occupation of German trenches, but this time our platoon was unscathed. It was unbelievably all over and this part of the ridge was ours. I sent Wilson, the platoon runner, back to Major Bridgman to report success.

Our other two platoons had meanwhile driven back the original enemy attack, so the remaining task for our company was to move higher up the ridge on our left to take over from the Irish Guards. Here we found a tragic scene. The Guards who had been the spearhead of the whole offensive had succeeded in defeating the enemy, but at a terrible cost. The steep slopes below were littered with their dead bodies. Others lay beneath mounds of earth and rock with only a temporary wooden cross and steel helmet to recall their heroic endurance. The few who remained alive welcomed us silently for they were too dazed and exhausted to say much. We waved farewell to them as they made their way wearily down the steep track.

For the rest of the day we remained unmolested except for spasmodic shelling which appeared to be aimed mainly at the transport bringing up food, water and supplies. Down below, the valley looked arid and dusty; the enemy was not to be seen, but in the distance we could hear the rumblings of vehicles and tanks, no doubt bringing up reinforcements and ammunition.

Soon after midnight came a new outburst of shelling. The northern spur of the mountain seemed to be receiving a deluge of explosions, soon to be followed by the all-too-familiar sight of tracer bullets weaving fiery patterns across each other. For several hours this new battle continued, but we who were not directly involved could only wait and hope.

By dawn, the conflict had mainly died down, but it was not until the afternoon that we heard what had happened. Major Bridgman called for his three platoon commanders. Like all of us, his eyes were drawn from lack of sleep, but he greeted us as cheerfully as usual. 'Welcome to our new home on the mountain,' he began. 'As you can guess from all the fireworks last night, the Germans have re-occupied the forward spur. So we have to drive them off all over again. This time the task will fall to the 3rd Brigade. The Brigadier has thought up a brilliant plan. After dark the whole Brigade will march across the two miles of open plains and hide up in the dense scrub at the foot of the mountain. They will have to wait there all morning until at exactly 2.15 the RAF will bomb that part of the mountain held by the enemy. As their target is less than a mile away, we shall have to light flares to show our position – please don't bomb us!' He signed to an orderly to produce a box containing the flares which were distributed to each platoon. 'These orange flares have to be lit three times at intervals of exactly six minutes. Then after the bombing will come an artillery barrage followed by the infantry swarming out of the bushes and up the mountain. Meanwhile our whole battalion will keep up continual fire from our different positions to make the enemy think the attack will come from us.'

For the rest of the day and all night long a series of fire-bursts came from all our companies under a carefully devised schedule. The Germans replied spasmodically, but seemed confused as our fire came from many different parts of the mountain.

At dawn the next morning we looked anxiously down to the valley below to see where the 3rd Brigade was lying. At first I could see nothing but the dry sun-baked earth and brown stunted scrub. Then through my field glasses I could just make out the camouflaged forms of men lying motionless in the foothills and wadis, all merging into the scrub and shadows. Somewhere in this small area nearly 3,000 men were hiding with all their weapons, and the enemy in great strength some 1,000 feet above!

All that morning nothing happened, except for occasional shelling on our ridge. Then at exactly 2.15, we lit our flares just as the roar of bombers came from the west. Two RAF squadrons flew over the mountain. We saw the bombs fall and explode with a tremendous blast exactly on the enemy positions.

Each time we lit our flares two more squadrons arrived and dropped their bombs. The sky was pitted with smoke puffs from the German AA batteries, but not one of our planes wavered from its course. Then, as though all this was not sufficient, a tremendous barrage from our heavy guns pounded the enemy strongholds. The air was filled with continual high-pitched wails and deep roaring thunder.

At last, at five o'clock, the foothills and wadis beneath us became alive. From my commanding viewpoint I watched amazed as out of the barren earth hundreds of men began to move. It seemed as though the arid wadis had suddenly turned into men and were beginning to creep up the steep mountain side. The roar of artillery had ceased and given place to the rattle of machine guns. The final battle for the Bou Aoukaz had begun.

When darkness fell, fighting was taking place on all the rocky summits and ridges of the mountain. The three battalions of the 3rd Brigade – the Duke of Wellingtons, the KSLI and the Sherwood Forresters were all in the thick of it.

At midnight I received a message, 'Stand by to resist enemy counter-attack along your ridge.' For an hour we waited anxiously in the darkness. Then came another message, 'Be prepared to attack Point 226.' This was a spur at the highest point of this part of the area. It was not until the first sign of dawn that we finally got the order to move. No response came from the enemy. We reached the top of Point 226 to find a series of empty trenches. In one which I jumped into I found a bottle of German wine and a fine pair of Zeiss binoculars (which I still have). The Germans had left in a hurry, but we realised what a strong defensive position they had been forced to abandon.

Then as the light increased I was able to see right over the wide plains to the east for many miles. The sounds of fighting on our mountain had died down but instead, a new and overwhelming artillery barrage had started from behind the westerly hills, while the plains beneath us were erupting beneath a tremendous shattering of shells. This, I realised, must surely be the great combined offensive to defeat all the Axis forces and capture Tunis.

From our mountain eyrie we had the most amazing view as the opening stages of the battle began. Although we were not at the time conversant with all that had been happening on other fronts, we later heard the full dramatic story – which needs a chapter to itself.

5
Montgomery v Rommel

In mid-March 1943, General Montgomery had launched his offensive against Rommel's formidable Mareth Line, which stretched inland from the Gulf of Gabes, about a hundred miles south of Sfax. Before the battle, Rommel addressed his troops warning them that if they failed to repel the Eighth Army the days of the Axis forces in North Africa were numbered. Then in order to force the initiative, Rommel tried to pre-empt our attack by repeating the tactics he had so successfully employed in France in 1940; by using his armour as a spearhead against or round the British flank, destroying our tanks and then dealing with the infantry. Unfortunately for Rommel, he had greatly underestimated the strength of the British defences and was severely repulsed, losing over 50 tanks and many men. He was recalled to Europe by Hitler, supposedly on the grounds of ill-health, leaving General Messe commanding the divisions in the south, while General von Arnim took over command of all Axis forces in North Africa.

General Montgomery's plan was based on two main elements – a coastal attack on the Mareth Line by the 50th and 51st Divisions, followed by his now famous 'left hook' round the German flank by British armour and the New Zealand infantry. These tactics, after a hard fought battle on all fronts, were completely successful. The strongly defended Mareth Line was outflanked and Rommel was again forced to retreat.

Meanwhile, near Gafsa, about ninety miles to the north-west, the 10th Panzer Division, with over 50 tanks, attacked the US 1st Armoured Division. After a brilliantly fought tank battle the US forces destroyed 20 German tanks while the 1st and 9th US Infantry Divisions went into the attack and took many prisoners.

The trap round the Axis forces was gradually closing, as the retreating enemy set up a new line at Wadi Akarit on the coast. This was an ideal defensive position astride a deep canyon, strongly fortified with mines, wire and tanks. Montgomery decided on a frontal attack with the Highland, Indian and 50th Divisions. In a fierce moonlight assault, the attackers made six main penetrations through which the 1st Armoured Division and the New Zealanders forced their way, while the Western Desert Air Force mounted a 'pursuit blitz' on the retreating enemy.

The Eighth Army continued to move northwards. On 8 April their forward troops met with the victorious US Corps south of Gafsa. The contrast between the two armies was great. The Eighth Army soldiers were deeply tanned, dusty and ragged, with honourable scars – and victorious! The Americans, confident with their recent successes, were efficient, extremely well equipped, and smartly dressed, with almost new vehicles. The British and US forces thus formed a quickly advancing threat to the Axis from the south, swarming past the huge Roman amphitheatre of El Djem and the holy city of Kairouan.

By now the Germans had lost about 30,000 men killed, wounded or taken prisoner. Many of their guns had been captured, while the Royal Navy and the RAF had sunk many Axis ships bringing vital petrol and stores to the beleaguered army. On the credit side for the Germans, the two armies of General Messe in the south and von Arnim's in Tunisia came together to form a huge defensive ring around Tunis, from Kef Abbed west of Bizerta on the north coast round to the east coast at Enfidaville.

Montgomery's original plan was to make a frontal attack from Enfidaville with the Armoured Brigade, the 50th and the New Zealand Divisions, who would fight their way up the coastal plain, no doubt suffering many casualties. General Brian Horrocks, who had been in command of the mobile 10 Corps, was called to the Eighth Army HQ. As he writes (in his book *A Full Life* p.166):

> Inside the caravan were Generals Alexander and Montgomery standing in front of a map. Monty turned to me and said: 'The whole weight of the final attack is being shifted from here round to the 1st Army front. You will go off today, taking with you the 4th Indian Division, 7th Armoured Division and 201st Guards Brigade, and you will assume command of the 9th Corps in General Anderson's army. You will then smash through to Tunis and finish the war in North Africa.

Now that Montgomery had rearranged his forces, General Alexander conceived a brilliant new plan to catch the enemy on the wrong foot. In addition to some of the British forces in the south, three US

Divisions were to be moved at top speed to the north so that the main thrust to Tunis was to be through the Medjerda valley. The 7th Armoured and the Indian Divisions had to make a spectacular forced march from the east coast, with no time to change the camouflage on their vehicles from desert yellow to mountain browns. As the Americans rushed north, the dusty roads were crammed with thousands of vehicles. The organisation by the staff officers must have been superb to ensure the swift flow, crossing at right angles, through the 1st Army lines. As a result, the sudden appearance in the north of the US forces caught the enemy completely by surprise.

The two opposing armies were thus drawn up for the final great battle. The allied line-up was impressive:

General Eisenhower was in supreme command of all forces in North Africa.

Under him, General Alexander was Deputy C-in-C and in command of the 18th Army Group, which comprised –

The First Army under General Anderson, and the Eighth Army under General Montgomery, and the US Second Corps under Major General Omar Bradley.

Air Chief Marshal Tedder was Air Officer, Commanding-in-Chief, Mediterranean.

Air Vice-Marshal Coningham was in command of the Tactical Air Force.

Admiral of the Fleet Sir Andrew Cunningham commanded the British and American Naval forces.

The two armies drawn up for the final conflict were like gigantic, lethal football teams. On the Allies left wing on the Mediterranean coast was a French Division, then the US 1st, 9th, and 34th Infantry Divisions, and the 1st Armoured Division. These were to attack towards the vital port of Bizerta, and cut off the German retreat route.

The British troops were to be the centre strikers, consisting of the 1st, 4th and 78th Divisions, and the 6th and 7th Armoured Divisions and the Indian Division.

Fighting northwards from the south were three French divisions, the 50th and 51st (Highland) Divisions, the 7th UK Armoured Division and the 2nd New Zealand and Armoured Brigade.

In their extensive defence ring, from north to south, the Germans were waiting for us with the Italian Marines on the coast. Then the

Germans could rely on ten infantry and three armoured divisions amounting to about a quarter of a million troops in strongly fortified positions nearly two miles deep.

Von Arnim issued an Order of the Day to his men, *'Behind you lies the sea; before you lies the enemy. You must go forward. You must fight to the last round and the last man.'* Based on this order the morale of the German troops was good. Although they were well supplied with fuel, guns and ammunition, they had little support in the air, most of the Luftwaffe having been despatched to Sicily.

All things considered the two armies were about evenly matched, except for two vital factors: surprise and initiative. Knowing that the Highland and New Zealand Divisions together with armour were in the south, von Arnim expected the main thrust to come from there. General Alexander's brilliant strategy of moving divisions to the north and centre had changed the goal posts.

The raising of The Gordons, 1794
(From the picture by W. Skeoch Cumming)

King Edward VIII and the Duke of York
inspect 1st Gordon's Guard of Honour

King George VI watches unarmed combat before embarcation, Jan 1943

| Cpl | Cpl | The | King | General | Major | Col |
| Boyes | Tripney | Author | George VI | Penney | Bridgman | Peddie |

King George VI and Colonel Peddie

Brigadier Moore and Colonel Peddie in Tunisia

Generals Alexander and Eisenhower before the battle for Tunis – April 1943
(HMSO)

The battle for Banana Ridge, 22 April 1943
(Part I – Chapter 2)

Seen from the air: German prisoners, Tunisia – May 1943

Victory Parade
Generals Eisenhower and Penney
4 September 1943

Royal Artillery (Ack-Ack) salute President Eisenhower
Victory Parade, Tunisia
(Part I – Chapter 7)

Attack on 'the Factory' – 25 January 1944
(Part II – Chapter 3)

6
The Final Offensive

Not even Zeus from Mount Olympus can have had a finer view of a major battle than we did on the top of the Bou Aoukaz. Following the intense artillery barrage, we watched amazed as squadron after squadron of RAF planes roared over the enemy lines dropping bombs on any targets they could find. The Germans responded with heavy anti-aircraft fire, but not one Luftwaffe fighter plane challenged the attack.

After the bombing came the infantry. Suddenly they appeared from nowhere. Rising from hidden positions in the thick corn, they charged forwards straight into the enemy trenches. As they ran they poured a hail of rifle fire to strike terror to even the bravest defenders.

For several hours we saw the battle waging. The men looking like swarming ants, moved on quickly from one weapon pit to another. As far as we could tell they seemed to be overwhelming the enemy, sometimes in hand to hand fighting and sometimes by sheer fire power.

Just before eight o'clock, as the heat of the day was rising, we saw the battle line of tanks swarming forwards. They headed fast for the gap in the enemy defences that the infantry had made for them. Superb and insuperable the tanks crushed all opposition. Looking down on them they were like an army of armadilloes passing through a sea of ants.

We were not left to be mere spectators for long. By nine o'clock orders came to assemble in companies immediately. On the move again, we could only guess our destination. We began to march down the mountain side while the whole Tunisian Peninsular was raging with warfare.

The great thrust towards Tunis was later described by the Corps Commander, General Brian Horrocks* –

> 'I never felt so confident about any battle before or after. Everything went like clockwork. The two infantry divisions

A Full Life – Lieut-General Sir Brian Horrocks (Collins), p.170.

punched the initial breach and at 7.30am I was able to order the Sixth and Seventh Armoured Divisions forward. By midday we were through the crust and the tanks were grinding their way forward down the valley towards Tunis. It was a most inspiring sight to see these two well-trained and experienced armoured divisions being used in a role for which they were specifically designed – to exploit a breakthrough deep into the enemy's heart. They worked like efficient machines, aircraft, guns, tanks infantry and vehicles each fitting into the jigsaw of battle in its proper place.'

LINE UP OF TROOPS BEFORE FINAL OFFENSIVE, MAY 1943

While the British forces were thrusting deeper through the enemy lines towards Tunis, another important battle was at its height further to the north. The Corps France Afrique and the US Second Corps under General Patten were making a fierce onslaught towards the vital port of Bizerta. Down in the south General Montgomery, with somewhat depleted forces, was attacking and holding several German divisions.

For several days the Americans had been pounding away at the German defences around the road and rail junction of Mateur some fifteen miles from Bizerta. To some extent the way had been prepared for them by the prolonged campaign of the First Army, but the knock-out blow still had to be delivered over very rough country, against a resolute enemy.

The Americans proved themselves to be skilful, efficient and brave fighters. Their first major obstacle before Mateur was a precipitous mountain of rock, named Djebel Tahent, some two thousand feet high, dominating the entire region, and constituting a strong fortress for the enemy.

During the hours of darkness an American battalion moved to the base of the mountain, while another battalion climbed up a steep rocky hill opposite, which the Germans had considered to be so precipitous that it did not need defending. At the first sign of dawn the US battalion was able to strafe the German positions with all their weapons, while the first battalion put in a devastating attack on the fortress. The enemy resistance was completely smashed, and many prisoners taken. As a result, General Anderson praised the American Second Corps as being a magnificent fighting machine.

The Corps France Afrique, aided with native Goums, made fast progress along the coastal region and captured the mountainous scrublands overlooking Lake Achkel near Bizerta.

We in the 6th Gordons, having reached an assembly area at the foot of the Bou Aoukaz, knew little of these events. The enemy was in retreat and we had to chase them fast. Our task, we were told, was to mop up the few remaining pockets of resistance and to prevent the enemy from regrouping and making new counter-attacks. So after a short pause for dry rations and tea, the battalion set out on a long march.

Colonel James Peddie, with Battalion HQ and a piper, led the way along a dusty road, followed by the four companies, each of which had the inestimable benefit of a piper. After several hours we halted to receive orders to attack an Arab village where the enemy were said to be holding out.

B and D Companies were to make the attack, but as soon as we got in sight of the place we saw that a squadron of Churchill tanks were already there and the enemy flown.

So on we had to go, hungry and thirsty, chasing an elusive prey, while in the distance the guns were still booming. The sun grew hotter and the road harder. Eventually we reached a group of senior officers, headed by the Brigadier holding a big map and waving his stick. At last we were able to flop down by the side of the road while Colonel Peddie conferred with the Brigadier. Then the company commanders received new orders which were passed down to us. We were to wait until nightfall when a hot dinner would be brought by B Eschelon lorries. Then our task would be to march to a village called Chaouat and attack a German stronghold. The only drawback was that the village was thirty miles away, and we had to be there before dawn!

On the march again, but at least we had had a hot dinner of stew. Our feet were sore before we even started, and the night was sultry, clouds hiding the stars. All night we marched too tired to wonder what reception we should get. Shortly before dawn we were halted. Word came back that the bridge over the river at Djedeida had been blown so we should have to go back on our tracks, make a detour and cross the river at a ford.

The load on our backs became heavier and heavier as we left the road and followed the river bank until rippling shallows made a crossing possible. The muddy water was only knee-deep and provided welcome coolness for our aching feet.

Then at last, shortly before sunrise, Chaouat village came into view. As we approached, a few desultory bullets flew over our heads, and a machine gun opened up from a house window. Our attack was fully planned and ready to go into action, when to our immense relief a white sheet was waved from a doorway, soon to be followed by other white objects fluttering from upper windows. The machine gun stopped firing and a white shirt appeared in its stead. We all cheered and ran into the village. About two hundred Germans emerged from the buildings and gave themselves up.

Soon a company runner came up to me with a message; as I could speak German would I come immediately to a chapel on a hill. Not far away, I saw a small white chapel on which Red Cross flags were flying. As I approached, a German officer came out, saluted and introduced himself as Dr Hoffman, the Chief Medical Officer of a field hospital temporarily housed in the chapel. He showed me round and led me to a row of beds beneath the altar, in which wounded men were lying.

'These men,' he said in perfect English, 'are all American soldiers. You see we have no enemies here – all are treated alike. We have all the equipment we need, but no water. We are desperately short of water. Can you please help us?'

'I wish I could,' I answered looking round at about a hundred wounded soldiers gazing up hopefully at me. 'We have been marching all night and we have no water either. But I hope a water cart will follow soon and I'll make sure you get some.'

The doctor smiled. 'We'll be most grateful, sir. It seems the war will soon be over in this part of Africa. Then we'll be able to evacuate these men to get the best possible treatment.'

I looked down again at the wounded Americans. 'Hi there – can you help me, sir?' A young soldier called out to me in a weak voice.

'I'll try. What can I do?'

'My right arm has been blown off. Would you write a letter to my mom for me? Tell her I'm OK. Tell her I'll learn to write with my left hand, and I'll be home soon.'

'Of course I will. Let me have her name and address.'

(The next day I managed to write the letter. Some weeks later I received a grateful reply from his mother. We corresponded every Christmas for several years. The soldier's name was Glen Mason of Manhattan. He managed well with his left hand and got a good job after the war as a store salesman.)

There were about fifteen other American soldiers lying with various kinds of injury. Several of them asked me to write home for them, but they all assured me that they were being very well treated and given everything they wanted. Dr Hoffman seemed very proud of his hospital in spite of the shortage of water. He explained that they had been forced to move several times as the Allies' advance continued, and this chapel had been taken over as a final refuge.

Our breakfast that day came at four o'clock in the afternoon. I enjoyed three plates of porridge and several mugs of tea. The water cart duly visited the hospital and relieved their urgent need. Even more welcome for us than food or drink was the chance to take off our boots, lie down beside the road and sleep. For the first time since any of us could remember, we could, apart from the usual posting of sentries, spend the whole night asleep.

In the morning came the amazing news; both Tunis and Bizerta had fallen! After the overwhelming onslaught of the 6th and 7th Armoured Divisions, the first troops to enter the city of Tunis were the 11th Hussars and the Derbyshire Yeomanry. But no one would dispute that victory had come as a result of the combined determination and bravery of both the First and the Eighth Armies. The Americans too won a triumphant victory. Aided by the French, they stormed forward so fast in the heavily defended northern sector that they captured Bizerta while the Germans were too stunned to react to the final assault.

As we all cheered on hearing the news, a French farmer ran towards us almost weeping for joy. He started kissing me on both cheeks until I almost had to shout to be rescued. The joy of the local French inhabitants was quite overwhelming. The farmer brought his wife and daughter, introducing himself as M Antonio. If only the Jerries had not plundered his farm, he assured us, he and his wife would have killed the fatted calf and invited my whole platoon to a celebration banquet. We gave them hot tea, cigarettes and matches, which they had not seen for over three years. In spite of their warm hospitality, we had to leave them when fresh orders came to march on. Hundreds of Germans were still to be rounded up in the mountains, many of whom had probably not heard that the campaign was over. So on we had to march back into the region of arid hills, fervently hoping for a peaceful conclusion to our long ordeal.

7
Victory!

The complete destruction of the German army in North Africa had come about faster than anyone could have foreseen. The speed and determination of the onslaught by the armoured divisions through the Medjerda valley had driven a wedge between the main defences of the Axis armies.

Although the Germans had well-prepared plans to evacuate their troops by sea, if it became necessary, even this was denied them. Hardly pausing for breath, the 7th Armoured Division roared northwards from Tunis and cut off the veteran 15th Panzer Division, caught between them and the US 1st Armoured Division. As a result the entire Panzer Division surrendered without resistance. At the same time the 6th Armoured Division raced south-east along the coast to Hammam Lif and then on to Hammamet, while the 4th Division sealed off the Cap Bon Peninsular. The last remnants of the once famous Afrika Korps in the Enfidaville area were thus isolated and had no option but to surrender. The entire organisation of the enemy forces had collapsed.

It only remained for us in the 1st Division to roam through the inland hills to capture the many pockets of Germans who had been by-passed in the attack and forgotten by the German generals. To our surprise and relief hardly any of the troops attempted to put up any fight. They gave themselves up to us cheerfully, evidently as pleased as we were that the fighting was over.

By 12 May it was officially declared that all enemy resistance had ceased. Nearly 300,000 Axis troops had surrendered. More than 1,000 guns and 250 tanks were captured. Not even von Arnim, the Commander-in-Chief, escaped; not a single Luftwaffe plane was available to fly him to safety.

The celebration of the victory came on 20 May with a great parade through the streets of Tunis and a long procession past General Eisenhower. I, with one other officer, John Crewdson, was fortunate in being chosen to represent the Gordon Highlanders together with about seventy men.

The night before, the representatives from each unit of the First and Eighth Armies concentrated in an olive grove just outside the city. The march began at midday after we had formed up and approached the outskirts of the town. We passed white and cream villas gay with flowers, and deep blue and cerise creepers growing up their walls. On reaching the main street of Tunis, large cheering crowds gave us a wonderful welcome. Most of them were French, although there were groups of well-to-do Arabs and a mixture of indeterminate nationalities. All seemed equally happy. The men were in their best suits, while many of the women wore their national costume, and small girls were dressed in white as bridesmaids. The guns of the artillery and tanks faced us in a long line, their barrels dipped in salute. Flags were flying everywhere, and more crowds packed the flat roofs of the houses.

The 1st Division marched in one group, the three brigades marching in rows of nine. As the saluting base in the main square came into view, we saw General Eisenhower and other high-ranking officers on the rostrum. The pipe band broke into the Gordons' regimental march 'Cock o' the North', and as we drew level we proudly saluted the general, who was looking particularly smart in an immaculate uniform.

The march through Tunis was about four miles long and took over an hour. Eventually we marched out of the crowds and into a back street where lorries were waiting to drive us back to our battalions. We found ourselves camped in an olive grove near the coastal village of Monastir, a small resort in a beautiful sea-cove which was one of the few places which the war had entirely missed. In the ancient village the Arabs seemed to be much better off than those inland. They plied their trade of pottery and making cloth on looms that must have been invented many hundreds of years ago. Their small houses were whitewashed and sparkling clean. In the evening we went down to the sea and swam in the clear dark blue water, from where we could look back to the round white-domed mosques and the ancient high battlemented walls of the old town. Here we could buy oranges and figs, while resisting the persuasions of the Arabs to buy carpets or pottery.

For several days we remained in these idyllic surroundings. At night we enjoyed long interrupted sleep beneath our chosen olive trees. Our short interlude here was an idyllic as anyone could desire. Each morning before the heat of the day, we marched and drilled on the miles of golden sands, thus maintaining discipline. Then casting away all clothing we swam in the warm sea, had races and PT, soon becoming deeply tanned all over.

Always at the back of our minds, however, were thoughts about the future and where our next battle front might be. Sicily and the south of Italy were deemed to be the most likely, although Corsica and Sardinia might be possible targets. (In fact the RAF bombed Sardinia very heavily in early July, thus causing the Germans to expect an imminent invasion there.)

To our surprise, however, a new name was heard confidentially by Colonel Peddie who later briefed his officers – that of *Pantelleria*. This small island, a mere dot on the map of the Mediterranean, about halfway between the coasts of Tunisia and Sicily, and 120 miles as the seagull flies to Malta, was of greater strategic importance than its size would suggest. It formed an important enemy base for aircraft and submarines and was used mainly by the Italians during the worst period of the siege of Malta. Mussolini claimed it as his 'impregnable fortress' and strengthened its defences with men, ships and a formidable network of anti-aircraft batteries. Apart from its importance to the enemy, it was to be needed by the Allies as a vital base for fighter aircraft during the invasion of Sicily, planned to take place the following month.

To capture this island, we were soon informed, was to be our next task.

On 10 June the whole 1st Division was moved by lorry to the port of Sfax where we embarked on the *Queen Emma*, a beautiful ship which had served in peacetime as a cruise ship. At dawn the next morning we slowly sailed out of the harbour. The sea was calm and the voyage very pleasant, apart from the daunting prospect of attacking the strong enemy defences at noon. The objective for the Gordons was a mountain in the centre of the island which dominated the landscape. After troops from the 3rd Brigade had seized the harbour, our orders were to storm inland and surround the base of the mountain, while B Company was to make the initial assault up the steep sides. Not a pleasant prospect!

At about 10 o'clock, two hours before we were due to land, the island first came into view. Already dark clouds of smoke were rising from its centre. Then we saw wave after wave of heavy bombers flying over and dropping a tremendous concentration of bombs on the area of the harbour. It seemed as though nothing could survive such an onslaught. At the same time the sky was pitted by the bursts of thousands of anti-aircraft shells, but the planes continued their unwavering course, and as far as we could see, without being hit.

Just before midday we watched the first wave of the 3rd Brigade as they boarded the landing craft and sailed off towards the island. We were to be the next to land, so we assembled on deck carrying full loads of equipment and weapons on our backs.

Then at ten past midday a dramatic announcement came from the ship's loud speaker: 'Message received from the signal tower of the harbour – *The Island surrenders; repeat surrenders* – all troops postpone landing until further orders.'

A great cheer rose from everyone on board. The naval bombardment suddenly ceased and the bombers flew away without releasing any more bombs. Eventually when the clouds of smoke cleared, we could see white flags fluttering from all the gun positions on the hillsides.

An hour later further orders came over the loud speaker. We were to land at the harbour as planned, round up any prisoners and assemble at various points, soon to be allocated to different units. When our turn came to land we found the harbour in an amazing state of destruction. The piles of rubble were so deeply scattered that it was impossible to tell where the buildings had once stood. The few Italians who emerged from deep shelters looked shocked and confused and yet surprisingly cheerful. Looking up into the sky and seeing it clear of planes they exclaimed in delight 'Bom bom finito!' Gladly they complied with our orders and marched away under escort. Meanwhile we searched all the much battered strongholds, but they had all been deserted long ago. In spite of the bombing there had been very few casualties because at the approach of the planes, the whole population had taken refuge in shelters and caves in the mountains. Only the anti-aircraft gunners had remained at their posts, and they were well protected gun-sites. Nevertheless all of Mussolini's 'impregnable' harbour and defence positions had been destroyed.

By the end of the day, instead of hard and bitter fighting we were able to lie down where we were at the foot of the hills while the thousands of Italians were equally glad that it had all reached a peaceful conclusion. If only all our battles could have ended so happily for both sides!

The next morning we spent herding together more prisoners and taking stock of the island. Up the sides of the hills were endless terraces of vineyards leading up to a 2,000 feet high extinct volcano in the south. Owing to the igneous rocks formed from the old volcanic lava there was practically no grass or growth on the island. The villages away from the harbour and undamaged, had white cottages with flat roofs. Wisteria and bougainvillea, growing from sparse patches of earth, provided the only splashes of bright colour.

After organising defences against counter-attack, we were able to find temporary areas to spend the night. There was of course no shelter. Instead of our leafy ceiling of olive trees we now lay directly under the stars, while small waves lapped gently against the rocks below.

At three o'clock in the morning I was woken up by a messenger from Major Bridgman and told to take ten men of my platoon with two extra Bren gunners to the top of the hill overlooking the harbour. Bombers from Sicily were expected to pay us a visit at first light, so every available anti-aircraft and small arms fire was to be ready for them.

Within an hour we had reached the hilltop from where we had a commanding view over the wide harbour area. A quarter moon had arisen, casting a pale pathway across the sea. At the first glimmer of dawn the bombers came – about fifty flying high in tight formation. As they came within range they were greeted with a great outburst of fire from the ack-ack guns near the harbour. As yet they were too high for our Bren guns, but we waited hopefully while the planes dropped their bombs in the sea near our ships. Columns of white water rose in fountains, but the ships remained unscathed. The planes quickly flew away, only to be followed by another wave. This time they came in much lower, a perfect target for our Brens and rifles. We blazed off a shower of bullets up into their under-bellies. With shouts of triumph we saw black smoke coming from the tails of two of the bombers. Others seemed to be put off their targets for they veered away, only to fly into another hail of ack-ack fire. Some dropped their bombs into the sea, but nowhere near our ships. Two planes were on fire and spiralled down into the water, while three others looked as though they had been damaged and broke formation.

Once the planes had gone and the sun had risen we were able to look around us and realised what an outstanding view we had from this hill. Below us the steep slope was terraced with vineyards overlooking the remains of the white houses of the town. Before the war the harbour must have been very picturesque, set in the midst of the Mediterranean blue. Although the quays and the mole had been destroyed by bombs, our engineers had already enabled our shipping to land with supplies. It was of course these ships that needed our protection. Every two hours the enemy planes returned, Stukas diving out of the sun and dropping their bombs on the harbour and around the ships. The noise of their screaming descent was terrifying, and once again the harbour was the centre of a maelstrom of explosions and convulsion. Fortunately only a few of our small ships suffered minor damage, mainly owing to the intensity of the defensive fire.

In between these aerial visits we set out to explore our surroundings. Nearby was a much battered gun position that might have been used with devastating effect against our invading forces. Further up the hill we came upon the ruin of a large house, whose walls had been reduced to rubble. But surprisingly at the far side one room had somehow been protected from the blast. It appeared to have been the dining room of a prosperous Italian family. All the furniture remained undamaged except for a deep coating of dust. Carefully examining the contents of the room we discovered an attractive selection of glass, china and colourful ornaments. The family would no doubt soon return to discover the ruin of their home, so we made sure that this room, at least, should remain inviolate.

Sergeant Maclaren, who had rejoined us after his wound had healed, investigated further. 'Look sir,' he called, 'here's a crate of Italian wine, not one bottle broken!'

'Leave them,' I answered. 'No looting. We won't touch anything we can't replace.'

He looked cautiously at the delicate china. 'Amazing that these plates are not even chipped. Could we not give the lads a treat – have our dinner on real plates with silver knives and forks?'

'Today's Whit Monday. It could be our Bank Holiday feast.'

'We could take the table and chairs onto the terrace, near to our guns in case the bombers come again.'

'If the real owners of the house return to see their ruined home they'll hate us for it. We're the enemy. So at least we must share our dinner with them.'

'I'll get the lads to clear up the rubble as much as possible.'

For the next two hours every man assisted in removing the pile of stones, broken down walls and general debris. By six o'clock the ruined house was greatly improved. The remains of the stone walls had been neatly stacked. With the stump of a broom the dust had been removed from the dining room furniture and this one unscathed room looked as pristine as though awaiting guests. Even a few bourgainvillea blooms stood on the table.

Two men had been dispatched to the harbour to collect our evening rations – a large cauldron of stew with hardtack biscuits. We all gathered round on the sunlit terrace, cleared of all debris, which was by now a very romantic setting. The table was covered with a beautiful tablecloth embroidered with flowers and laid with china and cut glass. Wilson, who had assumed the duty of head waiter, served our stew with a silver ladle from a handsome soup tureen.

'How all the folks at home would envy us,' suggested Corporal Tripney, 'having Bank Holiday on a lovely island on the Mediterranean.'

'Or perhaps eating dinner on a romantic desert island, looking over the blue lagoon, while the girls –'

These dreams were interrupted by the drone of approaching aircraft. Everyone leapt to the guns.

Within a few moments the dive bombers roared down out of the sun. Puffs of black smoke from the ack-ack guns in the harbour spitted around them, while flashes of tracer rose up from our Brens. We saw the sticks of bombs falling in the midst of the shipping and a few on the hillside near us. At least one of the enemy planes spiralled down into the sea, but once again the ships appeared to have emerged undamaged.

As soon as the raid had passed, we hurried anxiously back to examine the glass and crockery – not one piece had even been cracked.

'I prefer light music with my meals,' observed Wilson, 'but I suppose the Jerries are doing their best to entertain us.'

The final course of our dinner party was tinned peaches, served out of a cut-glass bowl, followed by excellent Italian coffee. As though he smelt the aroma, we saw the Padre from Brigade HQ approaching up the hill.

'Good evening boys,' he greeted us, 'you look as though you have settled in for the duration.'

'Come and take a chair, Padre. Make yourself at home. Black or white coffee?'

'Out of real china cups? Is this a home of rest for old soldiers? I'll have white please.'

'What's the news Padre? How's the Brigadier?'

'In good form – just in the mood for a battle, he said.'

'He'll get it soon enough. Where do we go next?'

'Well, I've been told that our bombers have given Sicily a tremendous battering.'

Once again the sound of aircraft sent us rushing to our guns. No Stukas this time but a flight of low-flying planes gave us a perfect target. One of the planes burst into flames above us as a fiery hail of tracer bullets from our guns pierced its fuselage. Trailing smoke it weaved an uncertain course until it dived down into the sea. Other planes unfortunately scored a direct hit on a supply ship approaching the harbour.

This proved to be the climax to our Whitsun holiday, for no more raids came that day. Our life of luxury came to an end with a message from Brigade that the Division was to be ready to embark back to Africa. Before we left we made sure that every item we had borrowed was returned clean and shining to the dining room. We had hoped that the owners would return, but by the time of our departure no one had appeared, so we never discovered who they were, or whether they had survived the bombing.

8
Twelve Thousand Prisoners

The Arab village of Ghardimaou, about fifty miles inland from Sousse, looked derelict and inhospitable. The mud hovels which formed the dwellings were in utter contrast to the clean white houses of Monastir. The few Arabs who stood staring as our convoy of lorries passed were dirty and impoverished. Fortunately we continued through the village until a mile further on we came to a long high fence of barbed and dannert wire. This was to be our destination for the following weeks guarding some twelve thousand German prisoners-of-war. The camp was divided into cages in each of which two thousand prisoners were to live, complete with cookhouse and wash-houses, but no shelter. A German sergeant-major under the supervision of a British captain was in charge of each cage.

The surroundings were bleak; nothing but parched dusty earth, leading to a range of brown hills. Far from the sea breezes, a Sirocco wind blasted the plains, blowing like hot air from an oven until the shade temperature reached an exhausting 120 degrees. Even worse than the heat was an appalling plague of flies which clouded everything, penetrating our eyes, noses and mouths, particularly when we tried to eat.

As a German speaker I was given the special task of being in charge of the officers' cage (in a position with partial shade from a few olive trees), and also a big and very active German field hospital. This contained many sick and wounded Germans, together with a few British who had been taken prisoner and were still too ill to move.

On first visiting this hospital I was greeted by the chief medical officer who turned out to be none other than Dr Hoffmann whom we captured in the chapel at Chaouat. He recognised me at once. 'Ach, we have met before, Herr Lieutnant, after the famous battle of Chaoat! I hope your American friends are recovering from their wounds. We could not do much for them as we had no water.'

He then proceeded to escort me round the hospital as proudly as when he had shown me his chapel dressing station. It was clearly extremely well equipped. The surgery, designed to receive the wounded direct from the battlefield, was in a large double-roofed marquee, and had two first class adjustable operating tables, with powerful electric lamps, worked from their own generator. There were also X-ray apparatus, microscopes, then in constant use testing for malaria and other fevers, a sterilising equipment and many surgical splints and appliances. Dr Momper, the chief surgeon, was particularly proud of his chest of surgical instruments, with which he claimed to be able to perform any operation.

Usually I spent most of each day at the hospital dealing with the many administrative matters. Ambulances arrived at all times with patients from other camps. Funerals had to be arranged immediately owing to the heat, and deaths registered. Drugs and special foods had to be ordered, working parties organised, and the German Red Cross personnel to be supervised. Each day in the hospital work began at 5am. By 11 o'clock the heat caused all but the most urgent work to cease, but there was little rest for the doctors. Operations continued nearly all day. Dr Hoffmann and his assistant, Dr Gugel, worked with me in ensuring that all the essential work continued smoothly. One day a man from my platoon was brought to the surgery with a badly swollen arm and was in much pain. Dr Momper saw him right away and diagnosed blood poisoning. 'I must operate at once,' he told me, 'or he will lose his arm. Please, Herr Lieutnant, you must be present so that he will know everything is in order.'

Within a few minutes the man was given anaesthetic and his arm lanced. 'All the poison has been removed,' declared Dr Momper. 'By tomorrow he will be quite better.' His prognostication turned out to be quite correct.

After a few days the rather hostile attitude of many of the men in the camp changed. Perhaps they realised that this was not going to be a concentration camp. Life for them was severe but they were fairly treated, as far as was possible in these harsh surroundings. One evening the British officers were invited into one of the cages for a concert given by German prisoners. We were greeted by their Sergeant Major, who escorted us to reserved places in the front row, thus causing us to be completely surrounded by two thousand Germans!

Although we missed most of the jokes, the concert was excellent. A small orchestra accompanied several good singers and Bavarian dancers. Then for our benefit came a very realistic impersonation of Lord Haw-Haw finishing his broadcast. As the final item the

Viennese compere announced, 'And now in honour of our guests we should like to sing some Scottish songs.' A quartet of singers duly rendered 'Loch Lomond', 'The Bluebells of Scotland' and 'The Dashing White Sergeant'. At the end of the concert a very fierce looking Hauptfeltwebel (RSM) called the audience to attention and said to our senior officer, first in German and then in English, 'We wish to thank the officers for their presence here. May we dismiss please?'

In spite of the heat and dust, there was also some lusty singing at church parades. Our Padre always chose popular hymns and we did our best to enliven the dreary conditions. The prisoners also sang loudly at their own Catholic and Protestant services. Their regimental Padres are not officers but Red Cross stretcher bearers, usually with the rank of corporal.

The Germans also provided us with light music when a small orchestra came to the officers' lines to play for us during dinner. Solos were given by the violinist, who used to be the leader of the Dortmund orchestra, and a good operatic tenor. One of the prisoners was an artist who painted our portraits for the usual fee – a packet of cigarettes.

Human beings were not the only singers in this desolate valley. Nearly all day and night long, the air was filled with the incessant chirping of the cicada, like the wind in telephone wires. Occasionally a scorpion would scuttle out from behind a stone, and once an evil looking crab spider took up residence inside my pack. Another more welcome visitor was a praying mantis, sitting on my camp bed pretending to look like a dead leaf. He gazed up at me with huge limpid eyes and a baleful, pious expression, while he folded his forelegs in prayer.

One evening a far more extraordinary sound came from a group of Arab hovels outside the camp. Frightful, gruesome wails sounded as though some female was being horribly tortured. I turned my field glasses on the scene and saw an ancient Arab hag squatting in front of her hut, yelling in apparent agony, and tearing her cheeks with her nails. This horrible performance continued for an hour, when three more hags joined the bedlam, dancing round, screaming and tearing their flesh. We later discovered that one of the women's husband had been murdered by another Arab, and this was the funeral ceremony, combined with the awful rites for revenge on the murderer's family. The noise never paused all day and night. The four hags took it in turns to yell their revenge, while the native dogs added their howls to the pandemonium.

Our tour of duty in this prison camp lasted nearly a month, by which time we were all exhausted with the perpetual heat and the flies. At last orders came for us to prepare to hand over and move on. When the Germans heard of our coming departure, I received a formal invitation from the doctors to a farewell tea party in the hospital marquee. Until now our relationship had been strictly business; this, I thought, might be a good opportunity to see the German doctors in more relaxed circumstances. At four o'clock, therefore, I arrived at their marquee where all the doctors were assembled. As usual they clicked their heels and smiled. Dr Hoffmann ushered me into the marquee and showed me to a seat next to him at the head of the table.

Instead of the austere ration of hard tack biscuits which I had expected, I found the table adorned with a clean white tablecloth with china cups and saucers. Their cook had provided a variety of cakes and scones, no doubt made with the benefit of items from Red Cross parcels. The chief attraction in the marquee was, however, an electric fan which sent a refreshing breeze down the table. This had skilfully been fitted to the dentist's drill. The instrument of torture was itself dangling from the fan, while Dr Vogel, the dentist, regarded it lovingly from the other side of the table.

'Yes, we have everything handy,' he explained. 'If you get toothache in the middle of tea, you can just turn round to the drill for specialist treatment.'

'We are sorry you are leaving us,' said Dr Hoffmann as the mess waiters brought round the tea. 'We envy you being free to go outside the barbed wire.'

'Yes, but at least you will be able to return home safely when the war is over.'

Dr Schmidt, a junior officer who so far had spoken little intervened. 'Safety is of little worth during war, Herr Lieutnant. Death in battle is more honourable than being taken prisoner. Soon perhaps – who knows – you may be in the fighting again. That is what our soldiers would prefer, while we wish we could be with them to care for the wounded.'

Dr Hoffmann gave him an ill-disguised frown. 'Let us not talk of fighting this afternoon,' he said. 'Try one of these fruit cakes – a speciality of our cook.'

Dr Schmidt was not to be subdued. 'We welcome you, Herr Lieutenant,' he went on, 'not only because we have received fair treatment as prisoners-of-war, but because you are an honourable soldier like us. Soon you will be fighting against us again. It is a great tragedy the world has to be at war instead of peacefully benefiting from German Culture and the Nazi New Order. But while the war is on Germany must fight for its honour. It is the same for you British. Only you call honour 'sportsmanship'. There is little difference between the two.'

'I must disagree with you there,' I insisted. 'Perhaps it is because you can never understand the meaning of sportsmanship or freedom that we are fighting against Germany now.'

'Yes, you are right, Herr Lieutnant,' said Dr Hoffmann, 'we cannot accept your ideas of democracy, which we consider decadence, and you do not realise what the German ideal stands for, nor German culture, nor the concept of a master race. And because of this lack of understanding the world is at war.'

'Britain is at war because we realise only too well the results of the Nazi New Order.'

Dr Hoffmann smiled and paused while the mess waiter filled our tea cups. He was a pleasant faced man with fair hair and blue eyes, not at all the type caricatured in the war-time popular press.

'You mention the Nazis, Herr Lieutnant,' he observed, 'but I should point out that we are all medical men here, and as such are not Nazis.' (Here he gave a swift challenging look towards Dr Schmidt.) 'We are not fighting to kill, but we are here to look after the wounded and to heal. As you know we look after all men equally well, no matter what nationality. As there are no Gestapo here I can speak freely. You have a saying, 'The only good Germans are dead ones'. We hope to disprove this. We doctors have never agreed with some of the Nazi doctrines. So I hope that after the war you will remember this.'

'What about the pogrom against the Jews?' I asked.

Dr Hoffmann paused thoughtfully before replying. 'I cannot defend or excuse that,' he admitted at length. 'Before I joined the Army Medical Corps, I had several Jewish patients. They were good honest persons. I can only suggest that in the years to come the world will realise that what you call the evil of Naziism is not nearly so serious as the evil of Russian Communism.' He paused again, as though carefully considering his words. 'I foresee,' he continued, 'that in the not too distant future, Germany, Great Britain and France will be allies against the Russian menace. Perhaps when you get home you should warn your Mr Churchill about this.'

'I hardly think Mr Churchill will need my advice,' I smiled.

We fell silent for a few moments. Then Dr Gugel, a small thick set man with rosy cheeks, added a light touch to the conversation. 'It is a pity we can't settle the problems of the world here and now, is it not? I'm sure we form the nucleus of a very fine international conference. But your cup is empty, Herr Lieutnant. Waiter, more tea and cakes! Now please tell us about music in England. Is the London Philharmonic as good as ever?'

We discussed music and art until Dr Hoffmann rose and invited me outside. 'I would like to be able to show you round the garden,' he suggested, 'but unfortunately our roses are not as good as last year. Instead we can sit beneath this olive tree.'

As I rose to leave some minutes later, Dr Hoffmann added, 'Although we shall not see you again, we shall not forget these few weeks. After our discussions we may be able to enlighten our countrymen about the British people and your way of life. I look forward to the future and a new peaceful world. Now we bid you farewell, Herr Lieutnant, and good luck!'

The next day we handed over the entire camp to another unit, and departed in a long road convoy to our next destination.

9
Après Guerre

After those burning weeks in the dreadful valley of Ghardimaou we were allowed four day's leave in the delightful French fishing village of La Calle. One company at a time was taken in a road convoy over wild mountainous country until we came upon a fine view over the Mediterranean far below. La Calle seemed like a secluded corner borrowed from the Riviera, with sunny white houses sheltered by palm trees overlooking fishing boats at anchor in the harbour. The war had passed it by untouched, leaving the French fisherfolk to live their normal maritime existence.

As soon as we arrived in the requisitioned school-house in which we were billeted, we hurried down to the sea for the exquisite delight of plunging into the sparkling cool water of the harbour. On our first evening we found that a party had been arranged for us in the school-house by officers at the end of their leave. The invitation did not specify what sort of a party, but Major Lindsay Bridgman and I never expected to end it on the high seas! We found that among the guests were a group of women of indeterminate nationality whose presence no one could account for, but who seemed determined to ensure that the drinks flowed generously, and that we should all enjoy their presence in no uncertain manner.

Lindsay and I found this too overwhelming for our comfort so while the festivities were growing louder we managed to slip out and wander down to the harbour. Taking refuge in the only tavern, we were welcomed by several of the local celebrities. A party was already in progress, headed by Monsieur Antoine, the Mayor of the village, a robust and portly man who was proudly wearing his chain of office.

'Welcome my friends!' he exclaimed. 'You have won the war and saved our country. Pierre, bring more wine!' At once we were introduced all round to a motley collection of fishermen and farmers, all of whom seemed delighted to have an excuse to drink more toasts.

'My friend and I are really refugees this evening,' explained Lindsay Bridgman. 'We escaped from a party in the school-house.'

'Aha! very dangerous no doubt,' sympathised M le Mayor. 'Well you are safe enough with us here. But from whom are we to protect you?'

'There are a number of – er – ladies who wish to entertain us. They seem to have taken control of the school-house already.'

This was greeted with cheers of laughter from the French fishermen. 'You did well to come here,' declared Monsieur Antoine. 'Wine and song – without women. That's our motto.'

A cheer came from a dour individual in the corner, whose own motto appeared to be just wine. He put down his glass and beckoned to me. 'You can trust me, monsieur,' he said confidingly, 'I am a Russian. My name is Maurice.'

His appearance was certainly different from the Frenchmen. With fair hair and sallow complexion, he might have come from the Steppes of Russia. Taking more wine he continued, 'You and your friend and I are in the same difficulty. You want to escape from women, and I from Africa. So we shall help each other. Tomorrow morning at three o'clock I go as chief engineer in a fishing boat. You will come too. We catch fish. We come back and the women are gone. Then you will get me into the British Navy. No more fish, but great ships! Gentlemen, cheers for the British Navy!'

Everyone joined in heartily, congratulating Maurice on his new self-appointed commission. It was taken for granted that all the details were settled, while Lindsay and I were overwhelmed with thanks for our part in assuring Maurice's naval future.

Long before three o'clock that morning Lindsay and I were fast asleep aboard a small fishing trawler named *Plongeant*. When we awoke on deck it was already light and we were right out to sea tossing on the waves. A young fisherman whom we had met the previous evening was beginning to wind in the first haul. Soon a large net full of a quivering mass of silver was landed beside us on the deck. It was then time for breakfast. Another dark-skinned man brought up a pan on which a choice selection of newly landed fish was sizzling. With French bread and salt this made a very fine meal, finishing with a selection of locally grown apples, plums, melons and grapes.

Thus we spent the whole day, heaving on the choppy waves and helping to haul in the frequent catches. Only occasionally did we catch a glimpse of Maurice as he emerged from coaxing the little engine not to expire. Once in between hauls of fish he came and sat on deck between Lindsay and me. With a determined expression he declared, 'What I said last night was wrong. I never want to leave here. Already I have escaped from Russia. You must understand, my friends, that before the war my wife and I worked in a factory in Archangel. My wife was killed in an accident with unguarded machinery. The factory owners were criminally negligent, but nobody cared. Because I protested I was sent to Murmansk. I got a job as a mechanic on a ship, but life was harsh and bitter especially when the war came. Then one day I seized a chance and stowed away on a British ship after it had unloaded and was returning to England. After that – but I won't weary you describing how I was put in prison for three months and at last became an engineer on a French ship bound for Bizerta. We were torpedoed, but I was picked up almost drowned and brought here. I was the only survivor, so no one has missed me. Why should I move on? I'm happy on the sea all day with good friends and drinking in the tavern every night. What more could any man want?'

'Even better than being chief engineer on a battleship,' suggested Lindsay.

'Yes, but nevertheless I am grateful to you both for offering to get me into the British Navy.'

Lindsay and I exchanged glances. 'That might not have been so easy,' I said, 'so I'm sure you are right to stay where you are happy.'

'When you say that I am even happier, so tonight will you please come again to the tavern. We shall all want to drink your health!'

Towards evening the *Plongeant* returned to harbour loaded with many kinds of fish, including crayfish, mackerel, skate, octopus and one very large and fearsome-looking swordfish.

The evening in the tavern passed very pleasantly, all our new friends being particularly hospitable, while Maurice himself needed less solace from the wine bottle, having reached the decision that La Calle should always be his home.

The rest of our leave was spent mainly in enjoying swimming in the sparkling clear water of the bay, and walking on the cliffs, while the sea breeze kept the temperature to a pleasant 90 degrees.

On our final evening we walked down to the harbour where Monsieur Antonio, still wearing his mayoral chain of office, had assembled a number of his friends. We were introduced to the Chief of Police, a ferocious-looking man whose presence alone would surely have deterred any crime, the parish priest, a young man smiling and eager to please, and the village school master who seemed remote and withdrawn as though wondering why he found himself in this gathering.

'Now my friends,' began M Antonio, 'we are pleased to have with us two brave officers from the British Army. They have honoured us by catching a good haul of fish in the good ship *Plongeant* (cheers from Maurice). 'We hope they will be just as successful in catching the enemy when they return to the war!'

Much applause followed, while Pierre carried out bottles of wine and healths were drunk by and for everyone present. Thus on a celebratory note came to an end our brief period of leave. The next morning another long road convoy brought us back over the mountains and down the coast to the village of Hammamet. Here we camped in groves of lemons and oranges which grew along a bay of silver-white sand for many miles. Before dawn every day we ran down into the sea in time to watch the sun rising out of the water at the level of our eyes, as though we were swimming in a fire of golden flames.

The small town of Hammamet appeared quaint and romantic with palm trees and orchards flanking white flat-roofed houses, while the raised domed mosque dominated all the surroundings. It was only in the evenings that we were able to relax in this setting for most of the day we were involved in military exercises, including mountain warfare, and combined operations with tanks. During one week, six officers were taken by truck to the precipitous rocky mountain named Djerbel Ressas rising some 3,000 feet above the plains. Here under expert instructors, we were taught how to scale a jagged precipice and climb correctly from one crag to another, hardly daring to look down at the awful chasms below. Just as the moon was rising one evening, the most eerie and mysterious sounds drifted down from the foothills. The beat of drums or tom-toms mingled with some wailing instrument, while weird yells and screams made us think that a tribe of witch doctors were casting evil spells. We soon discovered that this was nothing more than an Arab wedding. Occasionally one of the wedding guests would suddenly rush forward and chase the bride, pretending to beat her with a stick. Then would follow fights, frantic yelling, with fun and jollity for everyone. Apparently these festivities would last for five days, with feasts and noisy processions far into the night.

The final victory celebrations in North Africa took place on 4th September in a ceremonial parade of the 1st Division before General

Eisenhower. For about a week before this event, I had been in hospital with a sudden high fever, caused, no doubt by the detestable swarms of flies. Fortunately I was discharged from hospital the evening before the parade, but was unable to take part in it. Instead, I with two other officers had the privilege of watching from a splendid position behind the saluting base, from where we could see not only the parade but were very near to where General Eisenhower was to stand.

We arrived early at the parade ground near the sea. We watched the impressive array of all the units marching into position, to music played by the band of the Royal Artillery, soon to be joined by the massed pipes and drums of the Scots and Irish Guards and of course the Gordon Highlanders. From our position it was like being at the Royal Tournament, with various Generals, French Admirals and officials taking their places, while other officers were waving flags and organising each other.

At 10am the whole parade was massed and ready. Over ten thousand men were drawn up by companies facing the saluting base in an extended line. The artillery guns formed a solid black mass, while the naked bayonets of the infantry flashed in the sun like a straight shining river. Then the cortege began to arrive behind us. First came two dispatch riders followed by General Eisenhower and General Penney, the Divisional Commander, in a staff car flying three flags. Then came the Corps Commander and his staff, all followed by a bevy of film cameramen.

The Generals remained in their cars as they drove round inspecting the troops, pausing once at each Brigade. The cars swung round and returned to the saluting base. Three flags were flying as the Generals stepped up on the platform – the Union Jack, the Stars and Stripes and the 1st Division flag. As I was standing immediately below, I heard General Eisenhower ask, 'Let me see, where was it I last saw the Gordon Highlanders?'

'At Tunis, sir' replied General Penney, 'and probably you also saw the 1st Battalion in the Eighth Army.'

'Sure, that's right enough. Now who's this coming?'

The first troops of the March Past were the Royal Artillery as the band proudly played 'The British Grenadiers'. Next came the guns towed by 'Quads', showing their massive strength. The Royal Engineers and the Royal Corps of Signals were followed by Infantry; first the Grenadier, Scots and Irish Guards, and then the 2nd Brigade – the

Loyal Regiment, the North Staffordshire and 'The Gay Gordons'; very proudly I watched Colonel Peddie marching at their head, his kilt swinging to the skirl of the pipes playing 'The Cock o' the North'. The Artillery band took up the music as the 3rd Brigade marched next – the Duke of Wellingtons, the Sherwood Forresters and the King's Shropshire Light Infantry. Finally marched the Machine Gunners, the RASC, the RAMC, and the REME, with four tall Sergeant Majors of the Guards bringing up the rear.

At the end of the parade, General Eisenhower asked for the three Brigadiers and the nine Regimental Commanding Officers to gather round the saluting base. He came up to them with a broad smile, immediately putting them at their ease. His warmth and friendliness was unique among military leaders – as I was soon to experience for myself. Seeing me standing with two other junior officers behind the platform he beckoned to us to step forward. 'Come and join us,' he invited, 'you have all taken part in the war.'

So rather hesitantly we joined the select group. Colonel Peddie smiled as I approached. 'You can be a colonel for one morning!' he suggested.

'Well gentlemen,' the General began, 'that was a mighty fine sight! You don't often see a fighting Division giving a display like this. It has given me very much pleasure and pride. Also it gives us confidence for the future: you have shown the remarkable strength and efficiency of the Division and a high standard of training, equipment and fitness. But as I see it, the finest promise for the Allies is that you have invited an American Commander-in-Chief to take the salute of your troops. That Commander-in-Chief is now feeling just as much pride in your excellence as he would in seeing his own troops from way back in Texas. I think that Hitler will be feeling very anxious when he realises just how well the British and American forces can fight together. In spite of many differences in tradition, training and battle experience, our two armies have welded remarkably well together. Maybe some personalities have clashed and opinions differed – we are all only human – but somehow we have overcome all these difficulties and together we have conquered the enemy. We shall fight on together and win the war! Thank you, gentlemen.'

What the General did not say was that he was the only leader capable of uniting our two nations so effectively into a workable team. This was his particular genius. Realising that commanders such as Patton, Bradley and Montgomery had had more battle experience, he delegated much to them while he kept the reins and drove his team to victory. Two months later Winston Churchill, while visiting Malta, met Generals Eisenhower and Alexander. In his book (*The Second World War*, Vol V) Churchill wrote, 'After the conclusion of the Tunisian campaign I had suggested to the King that General Alexander should receive the distinction of the North Africa ribbon with the numerals 1 and 8 upon it, representing the two victorious British armies of the campaign. I felt that as Eisenhower had been the Supreme Commander this was also his by right, and I sought and obtained the King's approval. I had the honour of investing these two Commanders with this unique decoration. They were both taken by surprise, and seemed highly gratified when I pinned the ribbons on their coats.'

After talking to some of the other senior officers, General Eisenhower stepped into his car and drove off. As he passed a crowd of cheering troops he took off his hat and shouted 'Good luck boys!' So ended a memorable day; although I had missed taking part in the parade, I was more than happy to have witnessed it from beside the saluting base, and to have been one of the very few to have heard General Eisenhower's talk.

During the next few weeks, as an interlude to our intensive mountain warfare manoeuvres, some of us took the opportunity to visit the city of Tunis. Already much had been done to restore its life and prosperity. Shops and cafes reopened, while the streets were busy with army trucks and jeeps. In the shade of the palm trees the pavements were thronged with sight-seeing troops, French people shopping and Arabs selling fruit, flowers and trinkets. The native bazaars were colourful with all kinds of imitation jewellery, glass, china and souvenirs at extortionate prices. Nearby Italian and French shops exhibited bright silk scarves and shawls, and a large selection of beautiful oriental rings and carpets. In the evening we enjoyed an excellent dinner in the Majestic Hotel, taken over as an officers' club, as it had been for the German officers. The same orchestra that had entertained the Germans, played to us with complete impartiality such favourites as 'Lilli Marlene', and German and British folk songs.

On another occasion we were fortunate to get transport to Tunis to hear a recital in the Tunis Opera House by Solomon who had flown over from England to play to the Forces. He was given a tremendous reception by a house packed with troops. He looked very pale beside everyone else's dark brown faces. For nearly two hours we sat enraptured as he played Brahms, Chopin and the Moonlight Sonata.

For two months we continued with our training, sometimes in exercises with tanks (how valuable these proved to be in later battles), but mostly with manoeuvres in mountain warfare. The first signs of the African autumn came before dawn one morning in October. We were on a five day exercise in the mountains when the long dry season was shattered by a great thunderstorm with torrential rain and floods, while the Mediterranean was whipped into sudden fury by the storm. I had made my temporary bed on top of a six-foot wide wall of a long forgotten Roman ruin, but many of the others had dossed down in a deep wadi, with the result that many sleeping beauties were nearly swept away by flood water rushing down from the hills. By sunrise the storm had moved on, although summer lightning still flashed out to sea. Before the exercise ended, came the first welcome signs of new grass sprouting where dust had lain thick for so long, while on the hillsides thyme, rosemary and tall bell heather were surrounded by yellow aconites and pale autumn crocus.

One morning after we had 'captured' a few mountains, we came to a desolate pass, guarded by tall rocky crags. In the centre of this we found a small community of Arabs living in complete isolation. In this rocky terrain it was difficult to see how they lived. Dark clothed women were drawing water from wells, surrounded by herds of goats, while men were swearing at their camels. As we approached the camels took fright and ran away, while the Arabs stood stupefied with amazement. To these primitive people the sight of a hundred men armed with rifles, Bren guns and mortars must have seemed like an invasion from Mars. We waved to them in a friendly manner and moved on to round up the mock enemy.

In this part of Africa it seemed that instead of autumn there were two seasons of spring. After the rain, the earth which has been parched and arid for so many months awoke anew. Grass returned to the hills mingled with spring-like flowers, while many-coloured butterflies were abundant. Nearby the November lambs were playing in the sunshine, while the orange and fig trees were laden with ripe fruit. In such surroundings it was difficult to believe in war, but we knew that in Russia and Europe great battles were being fought. It could not be much longer before all our intensive mountain training would be put to the test. Just before we finally left Africa I received a letter from one of the men in my platoon who had been badly wounded on Suicide Ridge in May. It was headed St Dunstans.

> 'Dear Mr Grace,' he wrote. 'Just one or two lines in hoping they find you and all the lads in the pink as it leaves me at present. Well Sir, I am sorry I have not wrote before this. I am still blind, but they have taught me to type and also to read, and other things as well. Well sir, me and Chisholm have come here to St. Dunstans. We have got our discharge from the army, and they give us £2.10 for a suit of clothes, so they don't give much away do they! Well Mr. Grace, how many of the old lads have you now? Just remember me to all of them, and Sir, can you tell me how I got my packet, for I can't remember but my sight is coming back slowly, but I can wait so long as I can play football again. Well I must end now, so cheerio and all the best, Keep smiling as it won't be long now. From your No. 1 Bren, Johnny Cope.'

Finally we assembled in our last olive grove overlooking Bizerta harbour, heavily laden with packs, weapons and equipment, ready to march down to the sea. As the evening sun began to set, a flight of storks circled round overhead, and then flew off forming a perfect V, which seemed a happy omen for the beginning of a new chapter in the war and our coming campaign!

10
Christmas in the Italian Hills

We finally left Africa at midnight on 5 December 1943. After waiting several hours on the quayside of Bizerta harbour, we embarked in a small craft which took us out to the ship lying at anchor about a mile offshore. A choppy sea and the dark night made it difficult climbing up the scrambling nets dangling from the ship's side, especially as we were laden with packs and equipment. Several men nearly missed the net as a large wave suddenly lifted it away, but eventually we all got safely aboard.

The next morning we sailed away and watched the African mountains slowly becoming fainter beneath banks of white clouds. The ship steered a zig-zag course around the north coast of Sicily, finally berthing in Taranto harbour. The outskirts of the town through which we marched had been severely bombed, but the groups of Italian peasants watched us in silence, no doubt wondering what new disasters were about to happen.

We marched about five miles out of the town through flat cultivated country. Arriving at what was supposed to be a Staging Camp, we found that a generous supply of tents had been provided, but not one tent pole. However we were so accustomed to sleeping in the open that when a lorry arrived at two o'clock in the morning with the missing tent poles, no one bothered to wake up and erect the tents.

Two days later, we were established in a new camp on a fertile plain near the little town of Spinazzola. The nearby hills were covered with healthy winter crops, while the local Italians, although poor, looked remarkably clean and civilised after the Arabs of Africa. As well as a large, imposing college built by Mussolini, Spinazzola boasted three churches, three shops and ten barbers' shops.

With the prospect of spending Christmas in this camp, it was the duty of each company to make itself as comfortable as possible. In B Company we were now nearly up to full strength again, including four officers: Major Lindsay Bridgman, Captain George Reynolds-

Payne who had recently joined us from the Eighth Army, Lieutenant Norman Deboys, a newcomer straight from Scotland, and myself. It promised to be a most congenial foursome: George was a jovial, larger than life character who sported a wide handlebar moustache, and whose booming laugh was loud enough to alarm any passing stranger. Norman, on the other hand, had a rosy, boy-like face and quiet subtle sense of humour. Lindsay and I, who had been through so much together, regarded ourselves as being pixilated, and as such could see the funny side of things in a philosophical manner.

On our first morning in camp, the curious Italians flocked out to watch us drilling in the adjacent field, and then offered to help as we tried to improve our campsite. Unfortunately the complex irrigation system had not been finished in time for the evening thunderstorm. Down came the rain, while the thunder growled all round. The roof of our tent withstood the torrent but could do nothing to stem the river which was soon flowing merrily through the middle. We gave sighs of sympathy for the troops fighting in the mountains who had no shelter at all. After we had toured the company to ensure the men had somewhere dry to sleep, we returned to our own tent and curled up in our camp-beds, while the river was still gurgling underneath. We were like four seaside piers rising out of the water.

The next morning George was determined that B Company should be planned as a garden city with well laid roads and a proper drainage system. A squad of gardeners – we had a hundred of them – carried stones and gravel to make dry floors for inside the tents. Ornamental paths and gravel drives through the mud soon followed, while the cook-house was approached by crazy paving.

Inside our tent, a table was laid with a lace cloth which began life in Africa as a mosquito net. On this was a bowl of oranges and a tin mug with wild daisies and flowering nettles. By way of further decoration we arranged an art exhibition of our combined Christmas cards. Norman suggested publishing a catalogue of the pictures to guide visitors.

Our bathroom which existed only before breakfast, had real hot water. This came direct from the little railway station just opposite. The batmen took a canvas bucket over to where an engine was standing. The engine driver turned on one of the taps, the bucket was filled, the engine gave a whistle, several snorts, and puffed out of the station.

The final refinement to complete this home from home was the wireless. As soon as the No 18 portable wireless sets had arrived in the camp, I went off to see Jimmy Lecky, the Signals Officer. Very soon we were able to listen to the news through earphones. The BBC Overseas Service came through perfectly, and usually the Home Service station as well.

Meanwhile we did not neglect the comfort of the men. Their tents were dry with gravel and sand floors and we managed to take over two sheltered rooms in a cottage which served as a canteen with a large fireplace for warmth and cooking. The Italians entered into the spirit of the season as soon as they saw that we were friendly towards them. Women came with baskets of fruit which they offered at very reasonable prices. The men gave us bottles of local wine, for which they refused any payment. In return we presented them with matches, tins of coffee and sugar which they received with great delight. On Christmas Eve, a man suddenly burst into our tent asking for the 'Capitano' and brandishing a fine live turkey. Eventually after much excitement, gesticulation and examination of the unfortunate bird we closed the deal at the price he asked – 900 lire. The Italian then departed with effusive thanks, evidently delighted with his successful sale.

Christmas morning began well; the batmen brought us breakfast of local eggs and bacon, after which the old engine puffed into the station just in time to provide us with hot water for a shave and a hot bath in our canvas buckets (a bit at a time). After giving presents to our batmen, we went to the Padre's voluntary service in a large warehouse, attended by all the Company. To our surprise, we found that a small group of Italian men and women had decided to join us. As we sang the first hymn, they moved forward. The men who were nearest moved to one side to invite them to take part in the singing. As the service continued, there was one thin and wrinkled old woman whose face came to life as though she could understand every word. She had a black shawl round her head and a black bag tightly clutched in her bony fingers. A shaft of sunlight from a skylight fell sideways on her face, causing her to look like an old Dutch painting.

An improvised Christmas dinner had meanwhile been prepared by the cooks. According to the usual custom, the officers waited on the men on Christmas Day, so Lindsay, George, Norman and I took the place of the cooks, and served generous helpings of local turkey and vegetables, followed by plum duff, to the long queues of hungry Jocks. The feasting ended just in time for the four of us to listen to the

King's speech on our wireless set. Later we walked into Spinazzola village to hear the Pipes playing. This was the first time the local Italians had heard our Pipe band at a parade march. It seemed that the entire population had turned out to watch what was for them a unique occasion. All their earlier doubts as to our friendly intentions had disappeared, and now everyone was smiling and cheering. The men were dressed in their Sunday suits, with long, black cloaks. Most of the women watched from their own doors and windows, while the children ran excitedly up and down. Nearly all the officers and many of the men of our Brigade were assembled, so the crowds were very thick. At the end, when the Pipe Major marched up to the Brigadier for permission to dismiss, all the children crowded round so that he was hardly able to return to his band. The Brigadier then asked for another set to be played, so they started again to everyone's delight.

For our Christmas supper we four shared a small chicken that had been purchased locally, after four batmen, three Italian policemen and an old wife had chased the elusive bird all round the farmyard.

The evening concluded with a series of parties. First we gathered round the wireless set to listen to Big Ben striking nine. This was the signal for us to drink toasts to all at home, and to the success of our coming campaign. After this I joined my own Ten Platoon for a party of song and jollity in their tent. Finally I moved on to Battalion HQ tent, where Colonel Peddie was holding a party for all the officers.

During our stay in Spinazzola, we had done everything possible to ensure comfort and good cheer for all ranks. There was thus a big difference in attitude towards the troops now that we were overseas. Back in Britain it seemed that everyone should be as cold, wet and uncomfortable as possible – especially while at battle school – presumably in order to make us all tough! But now we realised the importance of ensuring every means of comfort and protection while we had the chance. This was one of the reasons why our fitness and morale were so very high.

So Christmas came to an end. Many of us would, sadly, not live to see another. We were now ready to move on and relieve those troops who had spent Christmas in the line. We understood that our destination was to be in the mountains beyond Ortona.

Boxing Day dawned with a powdering of snow on our tent roofs, and all the surrounding hills gleamed white and freezing. Much work had yet to be done organising the Battalion for its move into battle. In the narrow road leading out of the village a long convoy of troop-carrying vehicles were drawn up. On the morning of our departure, a large crowd of Italians gathered to wave us farewell. Women with baskets of oranges showered fruit on as many of the Jocks as they could reach. Children offered bunches of wild daisies, while the men waved and shouted

'Arrivederci. Buona Fortuna! Alla Victoria!'

After the lorries had been driving north for an hour we saw to our surprise that we took a turning to the left and headed due west. At the first halt, the officers were called to the front and informed that the plans had been changed. We were no longer to go into the mountains but were to travel under secret orders to an unknown destination. After a long and tortuous journey, we finally arrived on a lonely stretch of sea coast near Salerno, where the terrible battle against the Germans had so recently taken place. Little by little we learnt the secret of the new plans. The next fortnight was to be spent rehearsing for a combined operation with the Navy, the nature, time and place of which we knew nothing. The year 1943 had ended with the war in its most grievous and perilous stage; now we faced the prospect of new tumultuous operations against the formidable army of the Third Reich. We could only wait and hope.

PART II – ANZIO

1
The Prelude

From the wide sweep of the Bay of Salerno, a long trailing convoy of military vehicles lumbered slowly inland. Into the mountainous country north of Amalfi and Maiori, lorries, trucks and jeeps took a winding route. The lorries carried the infantry of the 1st British Division, including the 6th Battalion, the Gordon Highlanders.

Excitement and trepidation were experienced by us all, for we had as yet no information as to where we were going or why. For the past two weeks we had been carrying out intensive combined exercises with the Navy, being taken out at night to sea in landing craft with ramps that let down into the water, and then making practice assault landings on the beaches. All of this area had so recently been the scene of the bloody battles by the Allies to capture Salerno. It was easy for us to imagine the ferocity of the fighting as even now the whole area was pitted with signs of war – burnt-out tanks, wrecked guns and empty shell cases. The coastline was where the British X Corps and the US VI Corps had stormed ashore. After the Italian capitulation on 8 September 1943, hardly any resistance had been expected. But Field Marshal Kesselring, being forewarned, had acted with amazing speed. The 16th and 26th Panzer Divisions had raced to seal off the area and nearly succeeded in driving the invaders into the sea. The Allies were saved in the end by heavy naval and artillery bombardments and intensive bombing by B17 bombers, as well as by the superb bravery of the ground troops. As a result, Kesselring had decided on a phased withdrawal rather than allow his Panzer Divisions to be decimated.

Now our intensive training on these beaches was over. As our convoy passed through the scattered Italian villages we saw vast heaps of dust and rubble that had once been houses and shops which had been destroyed by bombs and shells. Villagers were even now searching through the remains of their homes. On some of the roads weary refugees tramped on and on with their few remaining treasures balanced on their heads or carried in ramshackle carts. The clouds of war had now passed them by, leaving desolation in their wake, while half-starved children looked up wondering if bits of food would miraculously fall from our lorries.

All day we rumbled on at the designated overall speed of 12 miles in the hour. To avoid being seen from the air, the convoy wound through inland roads, as though undecided which route to take. Towards evening after coming over a hilltop, the panorama opened up to disclose the magnificent view of the Bay of Naples, dominated by the pyramid shape of Vesuvius. In the distance we could see hundreds of small ships clustered together alongside the quays of Naples harbour. Further out in the bay, destroyers and many other naval vessels were assembled. It was a formidable sight. In the glow of the sunset behind the dim outline of the Isle of Ischia, some thirty miles across the bay, the arched coastline around Naples was ringed with shipping, darkly obscured in the lengthening shadows, and confused with cranes and other dockyard paraphernalia.

The convoy halted while the transport officers directed the vehicles in front to their various destinations. Then slowly we descended the winding road to the sea. By now it was dark. In the light of the stars we could make out the black line of the mountains whose snow-capped summits shone palely above the sea. Slowly we drove down to the small port of Castellammare, some fifteen miles south-east of the centre of Naples. At the quayside many landing craft had been drawn up, their black gaping mouths open to receive water-proofed guns, vehicles, jeeps and amphibious DWKS, while harassed transport officers organised their order of entry and positions on the crowded decks. Then finally we troops marched aboard, a company at a time, to assemble in dark holds and on deck to await orders.

So this stage of our journey was over. We were about to embark on a great adventure – or were we swiftly approaching Armageddon? We were soon to find out.

Brigadier Moore, commanding the 2nd Brigade of the 1st British Division, stood on a small platform looking down on the assembled officers crowded on the main deck of the ungainly Landing Ship Tank. Now that it was light we could see that some two hundred and fifty other vessels were slowly taking their places in the Bay of Naples to form an impressive armada waiting to sail out to sea.

The date was 21 January 1944. As we looked expectantly towards the Brigadier, we hoped that at last we should be given information as to the purpose of this huge undertaking. I glanced round at the other officers wondering if they felt as apprehensive as I did. Major Bridgman standing next to me gave me a reassuring smile; he carried great responsibilities yet he showed no signs of uncertainty. He as Company Commander of B Company of the 6th Gordons, and I as one of his platoon commanders, had been together first during our intensive training in Scotland, and during the past year fighting the Germans in Tunisia. Lindsay Bridgman was a man of great courage and devotion to duty. Although a strict disciplinarian, he was a father figure and friend to every man in his company. He imbued confidence to us all.

Brigadier Moore, with maps of southern Italy on a blackboard beside him, was now ready to speak. He was a tall square-shouldered man with a Roman nose, bright compelling eyes and a square jaw. He stood with an air of authority; no one could doubt his leadership and firm sense of purpose.

'Good morning gentlemen' he began. 'Welcome to this rather uncomfortable ship. At last I can let you know why we are here and our destination and task. As you know, the German Gustav Line extends right across the width of southern Italy; some eighty miles stretching from behind the river Sangro on the Adriatic side, across the Abruzzi mountain range and along the river Garigliano on the west side. The rivers and mountains form a formidable defence line. Hitler calls it the 'Winterstellung'.

'Five days ago our tenth Corps launched a major offensive along the whole of the Gustav Line. In particular, a battle is now taking place with an attack on the Germans who hold strong defensive positions on Monte Cassino – there on the map.

'This, gentlemen, is where we come in. In order to create a diversion and draw divisions from the Cassino front, we are to make a sea-borne landing further up the coast, some thirty-five miles south of Rome. You will see on this map there is a small port named Anzio, which is where the Emperor Nero was born, I'm told, and was a favourite resort of the ancient Romans. Our objective will be to land on a stretch of coast just north of Anzio, while the American 3rd Division together with the US Rangers will seize the port. Then we shall establish a beach-head with a wide perimeter, while the Navy continue to land tanks, artillery and supplies.

GERMAN GUSTAV LINE, JANUARY 1994

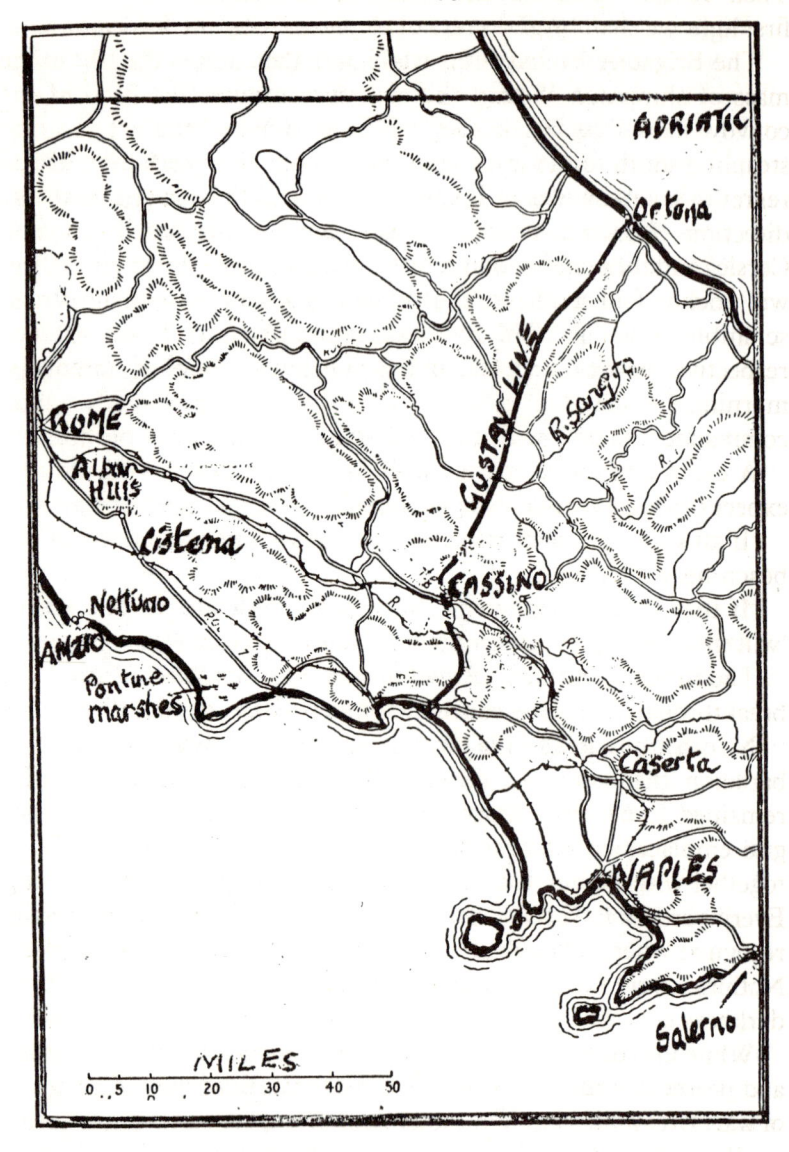

'Intelligence reports suggest that the Germans have two Panzer Grenadier Divisions in the area of Rome, so we may expect a rousing reception. Be prepared for mines and barbed wire on the beaches. But to eliminate at least part of the defences, at zero hour minus five minutes a salvo of over a thousand rockets will pound the coastline.

Then we shall begin the landing and achieve our first objectives. At first light we shall be given complete air cover by the RAF.'

The Brigadier looked at his watch and then across the bay to the mass of shipping. 'Within the next few minutes the head of the convoy should be moving off,' he continued. 'First we shall be steaming south round the Isle of Capri – not on a pleasure cruise, I regret to say. Any enemy spies in Naples should be misled as to our direction. Then we shall continue north-west in the direction of Corsica and then change course due east. By midnight the whole fleet will anchor four miles off the coast near Anzio. The infantry will scramble down ladders into landing craft to be taken to our respective beaches. Zero hour will be two o'clock tomorrow morning. I wish you all the best of luck! I shall now ask your battalion commanders to give you detailed orders. But first, any questions?'

A captain of the North Staffords stood up. 'How soon may we expect the breakthrough at Cassino, sir?'

'If all goes well in about two days. They should join up with our beach-head after that.'

'If they have just fought a major battle,' the captain continued, 'will they be ready to start another offensive so soon?'

The Brigadier paused, as though uncertain, and then added, 'The breakthrough will allow reinforcements to come through.'

No other questions were raised, so the Brigadier stood down. Each battalion then received its individual orders, after which much remained to be done. Maps showing an uncomfortable number of gun emplacements and machine gun positions had to be studied, together with the air photos of the beaches and surrounding country. Every yard of the area had to be learnt by heart so that we would recognise where we were even if we were landed on the wrong place. Nothing could be left to chance; the maps could not be read in the darkness.

While the convoy sailed on it was hard to realise how soon the calm and peaceful Mediterranean would be the scene of the stark horrors of war. Every man had his secret fears, but no one outwardly showed anything but cheerfulness. 'When's the victory march through Rome, sir?' asked Wilson the Bren gunner.

'Will you get us good billets in Rome, sir?'

'What will the girls be like?'

'Can we have some leave when we get there?'

'Will we have to live on spaghetti?'

Throughout the day the convoy sailed on unmolested, and as far as one could tell, unseen. If a German reconnaissance plane had spotted it from the air, the pilot would have given a very urgent warning; an immense armada with large troop carrying liners, destroyers and all kinds of landing craft, in perfect formation, gradually approaching the distant shore.

As the sun sank into the horizon, every man must have wondered, as I did, whether we would see it rise again. By the time it was dark we all had our final preparations to make. I studied again the maps and air-photographs, while the men checked their weapons and equipment for the hundredth time.

Meanwhile, a single destroyer passed between the ships. On the bridge stood the joint architects of the operation, Admiral Cunningham and General Alexander. The destroyer flashed messages of greetings and good luck to the troops.

By midnight we who were in the first wave of the assault were ready on deck to climb up a series of ladders and into the small landing craft. Each man was issued with two waterproof bags that would hold anything that would perish if we landed up to our necks in water. Beneath all the equipment, weapons and ammunition, our Mae West life-belts were bulging awkwardly.

Suddenly the ship's loud speaker gave the order 'Into craft!' One after the other we climbed up on deck and into the assault craft which were still on davits. As we stood crammed together in these shallow vessels, we could see in the light of the stars all the invasion fleet silently at anchor. The dim outline of our nearest ships were just visible against the sky. They would approach no nearer the land, but from their sides many hundred of the assault craft would soon leave to begin the invasion.

Soon a voice shouted from the bridge, the davits creaked, and we felt ourselves being lowered slowly down into the sea. Looking upwards our parent ship was black and cumbersome; it seemed as though we were leaving the last haven of safety.

A low rumble, like a thousand bees, sounded as the engines of the assault craft were started. Two sailors cast off the ropes. For ten minutes after drifting away from the ship's side we circled round and round, cutting across the wake of other caft manoeuvring into position. Then at last the whole invasion fleet was in formation, moving slowly off into the darkness.

It was now one o'clock in the morning. In exactly one hour we were due to reach the land – one hour in which to say our prayers, think of home, and imagine the enemy forces hidden in the darkness waiting to fire innumerable weapons as soon as we reached the land. Although we were four miles off shore, every one remained tensely silent, waiting for the time to fix bayonets. As the craft gathered speed, the bows churned up foaming waves. In the surrounding blackness these were illuminated by white phosphorous flames, brighter than the stars, as though thousands of fiery fishes were playing in the foam. On either side of us the other craft left pale white trails in the sea.

Vaguely in the distance the black outline of land came into view. It had no shape and no other quality but blackness. As the minutes passed this blackness grew in intensity; it seemed as though some long evil creature was waiting like a crouching panther to spring at our approach.

ALLIED LANDING ANZIO BEACH-HEAD, 22 JANUARY 1944

We remembered the Brigadier telling us that when we reached a quarter of a mile from the shore a salvo of rockets would be fired from a landing craft rocket, which was next to us. This was to be the first suprise in store for the enemy. Ten minutes later we were to land. It was not only the enemy that was to receive a shock. Suddenly a mighty flash stabbed the darkness and a tremendous roar thundered out of the sea, more powerful than a broadside from a battleship. A few seconds later, a more distant roar came from the shore. As hundreds of rockets exploded all within a few seconds, the coastline was shattered by flashes. It seemed impossible that anything could remain alive in that small area. This must have greatly added to the confidence of the troops landing in that particular beach, but we who were heading more to the north, could not help feeling that the noise would put the enemy on the alert for miles around.

Only ten more minutes. After the explosions had ceased, the coastline remained utterly silent. Were the machine guns waiting in awful stillness for us; the German artillery ready for the signal to fire; the minefields on the beach; wire obstacles to overcome? Four miles inland had to be captured before first light. All the engines of the assault craft had been cut down to slow speed. We were moving in with no more sound than a dull rumble, and the gentle swish of the waves. The intervening stretch of water grew less and less. We stood facing the shore with all our weapons ready to fire.

A slight jerk came from beneath, and the assault craft was grounded on the sand. With a clank the ramps were lowered. I jumped out into the water, about waist deep. After the first shock of the cold water, the men followed me ashore. Still no fire came from the enemy. The starlight was bright enough to reveal a series of slit trenches all along the beach. Not one was occupied! We advanced across the sand and found all the positions deserted. Beyond the beach a sand cliff rose about ten feet above us. Climbing up this we found a thicket of thorn bushes stretching as far as could be seen. After some minutes searching it was quite obvious that the thorns were impenetrable. The bushes were some eight feet in height, and seemed to growing indefinitely in every direction. If the Germans had been there to strafe the beach with machine gun fire, we should have been mown down, caught between the thorns and the sea.

Back on the beach I found Major Bridgman and C Company Commander. They decided at once to march quickly along the beach until we found an outlet. As we started, the enemy showed his first reaction. Somewhere a short distance inland a gun opened fire. We heard the shells whine overhead and explode out to sea, evidently aimed at our ships.

Marching hurriedly along the beach, we were suddenly halted by a single strand of barbed wire. Following this to a post, I found a notice facing inland with a skull and crossbones and the warning ACHTUNG MINEN! We observed this kind advice and went safely round the wire.

After half a mile we found a gap in the thorns and started our advance inland. Although intensely relieved to have suffered no casualties, we were more than curious to know why the coastline was entirely unguarded. The answer came when we reached what appeared to be a deserted farmhouse about a mile inland. A man ran out partly dressed in German uniform, looking sleepy and bewildered. Seeing our rifles pointing at him, he exclaimed 'Was ist los?' Quickly we made it quite clear what it was all about. Not at all reticent to give us information, he explained that a complete German division, supported by artillery, had manned the defences until two days ago, when orders had been received to move to new defensive positions further down the coast. He had been left behind to repair two broken down vehicles, and had been woken up by what he thought was a very violent thunderstorm. Our first prisoner was thus not only informative but even friendly.

After marching for a further hour we recognised several landmarks we had hoped to find. Soon we were on target and quickly established all-round defensive positions in case the inevitable counter-attack came before dawn. I looked towards the south wondering whether the American division had managed to capture Anzio harbour as planned. Although there had been sounds of spasmodic gunfire, all was now silent.

As we learned later, the seizure of Anzio harbour by the Americans had been a complete success. The US 3rd Division was commanded by General Lucien K. Truscott, a man of steel, aged forty-nine, who was equally respected by his own colleagues and by British generals. His Division was one of the finest and best trained in the US Army. Their target on this occasion was to surge quickly inland and seize the vital bridges over the Mussolini Canal. At the first bridge three German armoured cars awaited the invaders, but could put up little opposition aginst the armed might of the Americans and were quickly knocked out. That night however, units of the Hermann

Goering Division arrived apparently from nowhere and recaptured the bridges with a tank-infantry force. General Truscott ordered an immediate infantry counter-attack which struck hard and fast, securing all the bridges.

At the same time the harbour at Anzio and the nearby small town of Nettuno had been quickly occupied by three Ranger Battalions under the command of Colonel William O. Darby. The Rangers, trained for especially tough assignments, on the lines of the British Commandos, had been founded in 1942 in Northern Ireland. They were trained to operate behind the enemy lines and undertake the most dangerous missions. Originally known as 'the Ranger Force' they soon adopted the name of Darby's Rangers.

On the first morning of the landing the Rangers found nothing to oppose them but a few German engineers who had been ordered to prepare demolitions for blowing up the harbour in case it ever became necessary! A few other German soldiers on administrative duties were captured still in their pyjamas.

General John Lucas, in command of the US VI Corps was thus surprised and pleased with the success of the first day of Operation Shingle.

For the Germans it was a day of shock, having been assured by Admiral Canaris, chief of German Intelligence, that there was not the slightest sign of a fresh landing, as shipping in the port of Naples was quite normal. (It was a remarkable failure on the part of German spies that they had failed to report the fleet assembled in Naples Bay.)

Nevertheless Field Marshal Albert Kesselring, commanding German forces in Italy, was well prepared to deal with unexpected crises. As soon as news of the invasion reached him, his first decision was to create a buffer between the coast and the Alban Hills and to cast a cordon around the beach-head. The nearest troops for this were the 76th Panzer Corps, the Hermann Goering Division and the 3rd Panzer Grenadiers. To be the General with overall command at Anzio, he appointed General von Mackensen, a Prussian officer who had commanded a corps in Russia, and had a reputation for ruthless efficiency.

The opposing forces were thus lined up and the intensely bitter bloody campaign, in which the ferocity of the battles during an exceptionally cold and wet winter, rose to fearful extremes, was about to begin.

The few hours before dawn seemed interminable. It was a bitter night with no wind but a freezing mist drifting in from the sea. Our clothes were hanging wet on our shivering bodies, so rest was impossible. We stamped up and down to maintain circulation, almost hoping the enemy would come to provide some diversion. In the silence it seemed that nothing at all was happening, but in fact the essential build-up of the beach-head followed unhindered except for spasmodic shelling of the port and shipping, and three hit-and-run air raids by the Luftwaffe. One landing craft was sunk by a bomb, but otherwise the landing of men and supplies was completely successful. In less than twelve hours 36,000 men and 3,200 vehicles with all the necessary supplies were ashore. Altogether about 200 Germans were captured in the port area, many of them while they were still in bed.

As we waited miserably in the cold, we did not of course know any of these reassuring facts. It seemed as though we had been forgotten. What was the point of it all? What lunatic had thought up such a hare-brained scheme? Why can't we just pack it up and go home?

2
Churchill's Wild Cat

OPERATION SHINGLE, as the Anzio scheme was now called, had been the brain-child of Winston Churchill, who had been growing increasingly frustrated as the Fifth Army in southern Italy had endured four months of bitter fighting. Ever since the 3rd September 1943 when the Italian campaign was launched across the Straight of Messina, the advancing British troops experienced continual harassment from German artillery and attacks from well trained infantry. The cold wet weather and extensive minefields had made the terrain difficult for tanks, vehicles and infantry, even before they reached the main enemy lines.

Churchill would not tolerate delay. A position of stalemate was an anathema to him. Action, swift, decisive and dramatic was the only way he could conceive victory. It was in early December when a new plan began to formulate in his mind. The capture of Rome was the prize that would prove to President Roosevelt and Stalin that Hitler could and would be vanquished. Churchill dreamed of a great seaborne landing south of Rome to strike behind the German defensive line. He finally decided that the port of Anzio and surrounding coast was the most favourable part of the coastline to strike.

At the beginning of 1944, Hitler, too, was desperately in need of a resounding victory. His hard pressed Ministry of Propaganda could no longer proclaim blitzkrieg successes, and the German people were still awaiting the long promised turn of the tide when Hitler's secret weapons would bring final victory. If the Germans were successful in destroying this invasion the Allied plans in the west would be delayed and Hitler would have a few extra months in which to demoralise Britain with V1 and V2 rockets. Anzio had thus become a personal duel between Churchill and Hitler.

On 10 December, Churchill went by air to Tunis and then by car to stay with General Eisenhower at his villa at Carthage. The hectic pace of his life and continual worry caused Churchill to collapse with fatigue. Then two days later, Lord Moran, his physician, found his temperature to be 101. The next day pneumonia was diagnosed. Despite his protests he was kept in bed for several days, while Clementine flew out in an unheated plane to be at his bedside.* President Roosevelt cabled to him 'My love to Clemmie. I feel relieved that she is with you as your superior officer.'

Not even pneumonia prevented the old man from planning the war and sending telegrams to London. He was very perturbed. To the Chiefs of Staff he cabled 'The stagnation of the whole campaign in the Italian front is scandalous. The total neglect to provide amphibious action on the Adriatic and the failure to strike any similar blow on the west have been disastrous.'

As his fever slowly abated, his concept of the invasion at Anzio occupied every moment of his day. On Christmas Eve, Generals Wilson, Tedder and Alexander, visited him to discuss how they might obtain sufficient landing craft and other ships to make the seaborne landing a possibility. On Christmas Day at Carthage and for three more days Churchill and Alexander thrashed out their plans. The main objective was to force the enemy to withdraw divisions from the Fifty Army front. In a telegram to his Chief of Staff he explained 'It is not intended to maintain these divisions for long over the beaches, but rather to bring the battle to a climax in a week or ten days and thereafter to supply them from the Fifth Army.' He was not to know that the week or ten days would in fact extend to nearly four months.

By 27 December Churchill was decidedly better. With Lord Moran and Clementine he flew to Marakesh to recuperate. On arrival he was greeted with excellent news – the *Sharnhorst* had been sunk by the *Duke of York* and three cruisers. This news together with his activity on the war front had enlivened his whole being. As Lord Moran wrote 'As the PM grows in strength, his old appetite for the war comes back. He has a bright idea. He is organising an operation all on his own. He has decided that it should be a landing behind the lines at Anzio . . . The Italian campaign may receive a great fillip. Why, it may shorten the whole war. Hitler, I said to the PM, seems not only to direct the policy of the war, he even plans the details. "Yes" the PM answered with a smile, "that's just what I do!" '†

Intense activity followed at every level. When the various politicians and generals were consulted they raised many difficulties. The

---
* Churchill: *Second World War*, Vol V, p.377
† Lord Moran: *Winston Churchill: The Struggle for Survival* p.180.

logistical problems seemed insuperable. But Churchill with the support of Brooke and Alexander, overruled all their objections. When Admiral Cunningham commented that the planned operation would be fraught with great risks, Churchill replied *'Admiral, of course there is a risk, but without risk there is no honour, no glory, no adventure.'* That was to be Churchill's motto throughout the entire war.

So it was all settled; three weeks were all they had to carry out the immense task of planning, preparation and rehearsal. But nothing went as Churchill had intended. Before the Anzio landings, big offensives in the south by the British X Corps and the US II Corps were to have severely dented the Gustav line and overwhelmed the German divisions. At first the British 5th Division under General McCreery had achieved a brilliant success. On 17 January, with great skill and daring they carried out a night crossing of the river Garigliano in total silence and established a firm beach-head north of the river.

Field Marshal Albert Kesselring, Commander-in-Chief in Italy, was now faced with a very difficult decision. He could either rush his two Grenadier divisions, then refitting near Rome, to meet the offensive on the Gustav line, or keep them in reserve to meet any seaborne invasion. He decided upon the former, so the two divisions moved with remarkable speed and efficiency and cast a ring of steel around McCreery's beach-head. General Mark Clarke, the US Fifth Army commander, unfortunately failed to implement his promise to follow up the British success by sending reinforcements. The Germans were thus in a position to pour down an intense rain of artillery and infantry fire from the surrounding hills upon the unfortunate British. The casualties were disastrous. Kesselring had plugged the gap and kept his line intact.

In the area of Monte Cassino the focal point was, of course, the ancient Abbey and Monastery which had been founded by St Benedict in the year 529. General Fridolin von Sengler, commanding the XIV Panzer Corps, was a devout Catholic. He had arranged, with the practical aid of an art-loving major, for the Abbey's priceless treasures to be removed to safety in the Vatican. Then he organised the defences on top of the Monastery Hill in front of the Abbey, but the Allies fully believed that it was to be used as an artillery observation post and a fortified stronghold. In fact the ancient building which looked down upon the whole panorama below had a powerful effect on the morale of the Allied troops.

Field Marshal Kesselring thus had ensured that the defences along the Gustav Line and in the Cassino area were formidably strong. He still had to face the likelihood of a seaborne landing which might come anywhere along the west coast. Admiral Canaris, chief of counter-espionage, assured Kesselring that he need fear no Allied landing in the near future. This view was very reassuring to the German commander, for having moved his Grenadier division to the Gustav line, he had now only one mobile division in reserve. This he decided to move from the Anzio area a few miles down the coast.

Three days later the Allies landed at and around Anzio.

During the morning General Alexander toured the beach-head with General Clarke and found that all troops and supplies were better organised than could ever have been expected.

Back in London Winston Churchill anxiously awaited the news from General Alexander. As the success story reached him he signalled the reply: 'Thank you for all your messages. Am very glad you are pegging out claims rather than digging in beach-heads.'

For us troops waiting in the freezing cold before dawn, it was a rather different story.

The long night at last gave place to a cheerless dawn. The terrain which gradually revealed itself was a rough scrubland, with trees and bushes white with frost. This land had been part of the extensive malarial Pontine marshes until in 1928 Mussolini had initiated vast works of drainage and irrigation.

We had established our positions near a road stretching northwards from Anzio, and it was on this road that we received our first diversion. In the distance came the sound of an engine accelerating rapidly. Then round a corner a German armoured car suddenly burst into view. As it raced through our lines, we let off a hail of small arms fire. The bullets ricocheted off its metal plating while its machine gun fired harmlessly over our heads. It roared past us like an armadillo swarmed by wasps. We all cheered and waved our defiance. It was a musical comedy turn that helped to restore our confidence. (Later we learnt that the armoured car had driven on to Anzio where it was captured intact by the Americans with anti-tank guns.)

Soon a primus stove brought water to the boil and we eagerly ate our breakfast of bully beef and biscuits with plenty of hot tea. Once again we raised a cheer when a squadron of Spitfires flew overhead. Many times during the day the RAF showed mastery of the skies, while the Luftwaffe flew only twice very high above the coastline.

We marched a few miles further inland expecting the enemy to challenge us, but nothing happened. The countryside was barren and lifeless, the few scattered stone farmhouses evidently having been abandoned. Once more we were ordered to halt and dig in new positions. Our sense of futility returned as daylight faded and still the long expected order to advance never came. Instead I was given the task of taking three men on a reconnaissance patrol further inland. With few identifiable landmarks I had to rely mainly on compass bearings. The silence was oppressive; no wind stirred the branches, nothing moved. Only two owls hooted to each other in the darkness. For four hours we probed deeper between woods and empty fields. Around one farmhouse on a hill we stumbled upon a row of slit trenches now empty, that must recently have been occupied by German troops. Now there were neither humans nor animals. Thinking that the Italians must have had better precognition than the Germans, we returned and reported a deserted countryside.

After enduring another cold night we assumed that we would quickly be on the march. We waited in vain. 'They've sent us all this way to sit on our ruddy arses!' complained Corporal Boyes.

'We micht as well hae sent 'em a fucking postcard to tell 'em we were coming'.'

The men's opinions were well summed up by Sergeant Maclaren as we sat round a tree trunk eating our midday rations. 'By now we could have cut the main road to Rome and been halfway there. Nothing could stop us today. But by tomorrow, – who knows?' Maclaren was an excellent platoon sergeant, calm and efficient, well respected by his men, and a good friend to me. None of us realised how his words were being echoed and debated at that very moment in London . . .

Winston Churchill, waiting hourly for messages that did not come signalled to General Alexander,

> *I expected to see a wild cat roaring into the mountains, and what do I find? A whale wallowing on the beaches!*

General Alexander was equally frustrated. After the war he wrote, 'The commander of the assault corps, the American General John Lucas, missed his opportunity by being too slow, too cautious. He failed to realise the great advantage that surprise had given him. He allowed time to beat him.'

A similar view was taken by the German General Westphal:* 'At the moment of landing . . . the road to Rome was open. No one could have stopped a bold advance-guard entering the Holy City . . . The enemy kept suprisingly quiet. They were apparently engaged in building up a bridgehead. It was thus possible to build up a new front opposite them.'

Yet in spite of General Lucas being criticised for undue caution, he had at the time good reasons for establishing a strong base before risking inadequately supported troops. Both he and General Mark Clarke remembered all too vividly the awful casualties at Salerno, and were determined not to embark on any perilous ventures. Lucas was an intelligent officer, with a reputation for level-headed judgment and the ability to 'read' a battle once in progress. Lucas was acutely aware of the Germans' skill in reacting swiftly in a crisis, and in this he was proved to be completely correct.

While Lucas was engaged in landing supplies and ammunition, Field Marshal Kesselring acted with remarkable speed. Within twenty-four hours of the invasion, three divisions waiting in reserve in north Italy were on the move south, while other German units in France, Germany and Yugo-Slavia were mobilised for transit to Italy. Nearer to Rome other units on various duties were brought together as mobile reserves.

Hitler too had reacted instantly, sending a message to be read out to all troops:

> The Gustav line must be held at all costs for the sake of the political consequences which would follow a completely successful defence. The Führer expects the bitterest struggle for every yard.

Kesselring received some invaluable information when German intelligence intercepted a coded message (easily deciphered) to the effect that General Lucas had no intention of launching further attacks either towards Rome or to the Alban Hills until the beachhead had been fully augmented from the sea. This encouraged Kesselring to plan a decisive counter-attack rather than a defensive ring around Rome. At the same time the Luftwaffe intensified its bombing of the beaches and the shipping.

At the end of the day of frustrating inaction, I received a message

---

* Churchill: *Second World War*, Vol V, p.426.

to report immediately to the Commanding Officer at Battalion HQ. Lieut-Colonel James Peddie welcomed me with a friendly smile.

'Another patrol for you tonight, Ted,' he announced. 'Last night you went to these two farms,' pointing to the map, 'and you found nothing?'

'No sir, not even Italians.'

'Tonight may be different. Reports are coming in that a fresh German Division is arriving from the north. I want you to take your platoon and find out as much as you can. Bring back a prisoner, if possible. We need information. Good luck!'

It was a dark moonless night as we set out across the deep valley that bordered our positions. Every few minutes I paused to check the compass bearing, and to listen. On the other side of the valley, we came to a stone wall, behind which the black outline of a wood could just be seen. Climbing quietly over the wall I heard a twig snap in the wood above. This might have been merely a bird or rabbit, but signalling to the man behind not to climb the wall, I waited listening intently. Another sound followed, like a footstep. Then came the unmistakable metallic click of a rifle or a spade. Some German patrol must be up there waiting for us. I carefully climbed back over the wall to whisper fresh orders. Then leaving Corporal Boyes' section in their present position I took the rest of the platoon very quietly along the wall. About a hundred yards further on we found a gap where the stones had been knocked down. As we had practised surmounting similar obstacles so many times, we all climbed over these stones without making any betraying sound. Further up the hill, adjacent to the Germans' position, we closed round them on three sides in the hope of forming an ambush.

Then exactly as planned, Corporal Boyes' section opened fire, shattering the silence as though a far larger force was attacking. The Germans, caught by surprise, evidently decided to retreat. We heard them shouting and running towards us along the ridge of the hill. They were rushing straight into our ambush! I heard myself shouting 'Fire!'. Their shapes were hardly visible against the blackness of the wood behind. Our platoon fired a volley into the dark. Then followed total confusion. The Germans were on top of us, firing blindly as they ran. Then they stampeded headlong beyond us, without realising where we were, and finally disappeared along the valley.

Two men were calling out for help. One was Chisholm, our Bren gunner, standing just beside me, 'It's my arm sir. The bastards have shot me!' Hurriedly we cut away his sleeve, and applied a field dressing to the wound in his upper arm. Then turning to the other man we found he was a German groaning with a shattered leg. Again we applied first aid and tied up his leg as well as we could.

Somehow we stumbled back through the darkness, one man carrying Chisholm's Bren gun, and two others supporting the wounded German. As we were climbing back over the stone wall a sudden outburst of artillery fire came from behind us. Shells exploded with the intensity of an ear-splitting drum roll, while the low clouds reflected the continuous flashes less than a mile away.

Needing no further incentive for speed, we quickly reached our Company lines. Major Bridgman was anxiously waiting for us. 'Glad you're back Ted!' he greeted us. 'Any trouble?'

'Chisholm's hit in the arm. And here's a German – leg shattered.'

The Major called for stretcher bearers, and looked down on the German who had collapsed on the ground. 'He'll be useful as soon as he's well enough to talk,' he asserted. 'The CO will want to see you – better report straight away.'

Colonel Peddie looked up from his table covered with message pads and maps. I saluted and gave him an outline of all that had happened. 'Your German prisoner will be just what we need,' he commented. 'Not enough of them yet. Very little information.'

As he spoke a fresh outburst of firing came from nearer than before. As well as artillery, a tremendous clash of small arms and machine gun fire turned the night into an inferno.

'Get back to your platoon quickly, Ted,' Colonel Peddie ordered. 'Stand by all night in case the enemy break through.'

'Do we know what's happening up there, sir?' I asked.

'All I know is that the Guards Brigade are making an attack to capture Campoleone.' He pointed out the position on the map. 'But we don't yet know the strength of the enemy. It sounds as though the Guards are running into more than they had bargained for. We may be called upon to follow through. Please tell Major Bridgman to be ready for anything. And thanks again for the prisoner!'

I hurried back to my platoon as large drops of rain heralded the beginning of a thunderstorm. Soon the noise of battle was rivalled by the fury of thunder overhead and continuous flashes of lightning. The night became a tumult of crashing shells and the turbulence of the storm, while the downpour quickly filled out slit trenches with muddy water.

All through the storm we waited, cold, wet and miserable. The whole beach-head seemed to have flared up into a gigantic battle, while we could only stand by on the fringe, expecting at any moment to be plunged into the thick of it.

Towards dawn, the noise of fighting at last subsided. The storm had rolled away, leaving an unreal silence over a sodden countryside. As a watery sun rose over the retreating black clouds, I climbed out of my waterlogged trench, and went round my platoon positions. Interspersed with predictable profanities, the question was the same from every man: 'What's happening? What are we waiting for? Have they forgotten us? We're wet and starving!'

As though to answer, the fragile silence was once again shattered by renewed shell and machine gun fire.

'It's the Guards Brigade,' I was able to tell them. 'It's their battle, God help them. Our turn will come next.'

'Anything's better than standing all fucking night in this fucking water!' was the general reponse.

As we were later to learn, the Guards' nightmare was far worse than ours.

3
The Advance of the Guards' Brigade

The battle fought by the Guards' Brigade against the newly arrived 3rd Panzer Grenadier Division was one of the fiercest of the whole Italian campaign. It began quietly enough on the morning of 24 January when General Penney at last received orders to advance towards the tactically important town and rail centre of Campoleone. He chose the Guards Brigade to carry out the advance and ordered Brigadier Murray, commanding the Brigade, to move up the main road to the town.

At dawn that morning, a platoon of the Grenadier Guards was sent to find the enemy's foremost position. Under Lieut. J.M. Hargreaves, the patrol set out exuberantly, determined to let nothing stop them advance if need be to Rome. At a bridge known as the Fly-Over, General Penney and his staff watched the gallant platoon marching up a main road towards the village of Carroceto, about four miles south of Campoleone. In the early morning the buildings were silent and apparently uninhabited.

Beyond the village a tall square tower loomed over the surrounding countryside. This was the Town Hall of a Fascist agricultural settlement known as Aprilia. Out of the fertile Pontine Marshes the Italians had reclaimed an area of farmland, and built a model co-operative farm, together with a community centre built round the Town Hall. This centre boasted a church, school, cinema and shops. From a distance the square tower looked like a factory, and was known as 'The Factory' for the rest of the campaign.

The ensuing battles were described to me some six weeks later by a young Guards officer while we lay in adjacent beds in a hospital in Catania. I had been shot through the leg, while he had lost an arm and had a wound in his side. For a few days neither of us felt like talking. His name was Peter, but I did not ask for further details. Then one morning the nurse had left him propped up on a pillow facing me.

'Dreadful show that night I got my packet,' he muttered. 'Did you hear about it?'

GUARDS BRIGADE ATTACK

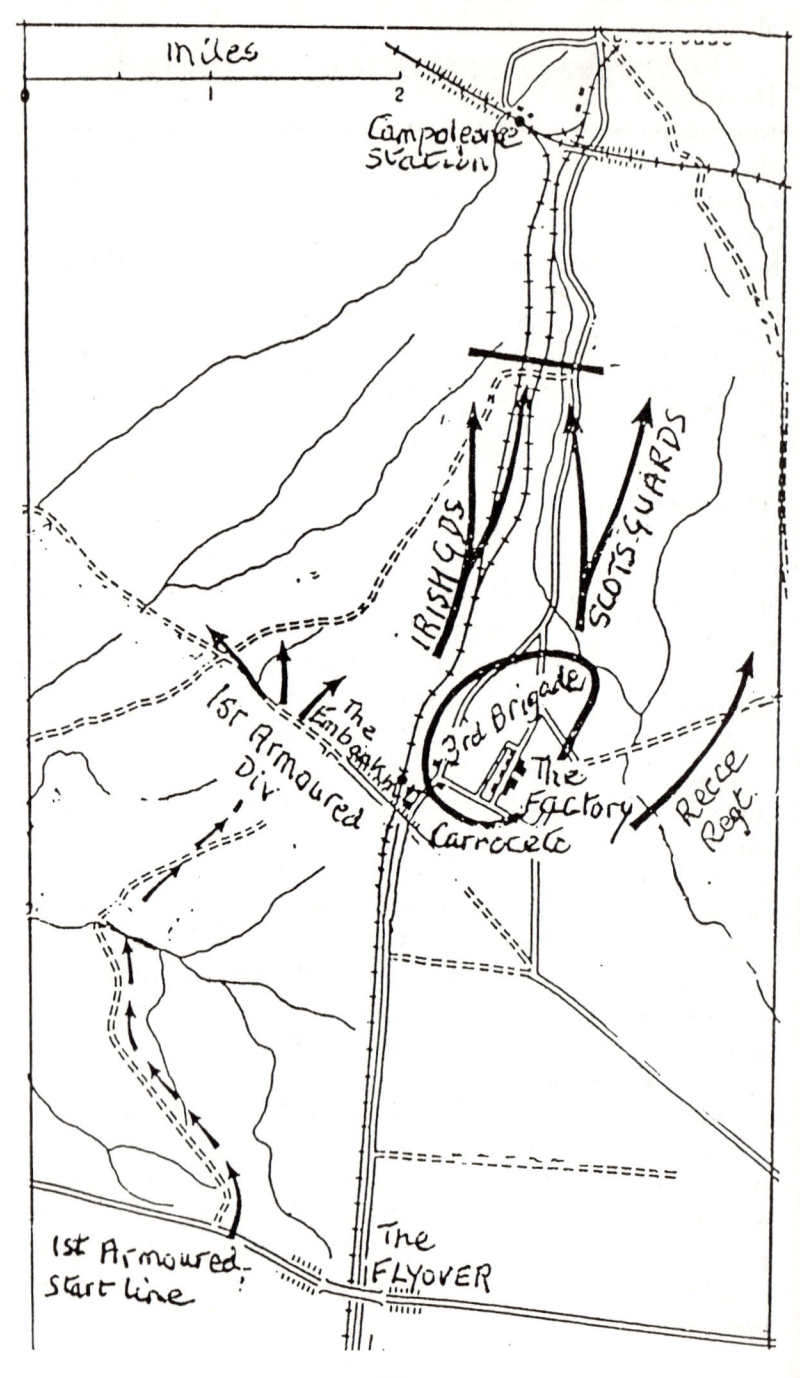

'We knew the Guards were in the thick of it,' I answered. 'Tell me about it if you have the energy.'

'I'll never forget. Perhaps if I tell you I may have less nightmares.' He paused and flexed his remaining arm. 'Our company was ordered to attack Carroceto village. My platoon was to give covering fire while the assault was to be made by the platoon commanded by a chap called Needham. We blazed off with all weapons at the village. Needham led the way over an embankment, over a wire fence and across open ground to the nearest buildings. We had to stop firing then, of course, as Needham and his men charged into the first house. To our amazement, about six terrified Italians ran out, their hands up, shouting 'Amico! Amico!' But then a machine gun opened up from a nearby building. Needham dived for cover and ordered one section to fire while he with the other two sections attacked from one side. Great chap Needham! A grenade settled the machine gun. They soon captured all the other houses.' Peter paused, out of breath. He shut his eyes and seemed to fall into a deep sleep.

The next morning after the surgeon's visit, Peter seemed stronger. 'Slept better after talking to you,' he said. 'But the worst part is to come.' He took a sip of water from his tray and continued, 'That afternoon we were ordered to attack the Factory. First the artillery put down a barrage on the buildings – should have knocked the stuffing out of them. Then a smoke screen was laid down. Our company with B Company charged down from the embankment. But the wind blew away the smoke and we were sitting – or rather, running ducks. Before we got to the first building a rain of machine gun fire swept into us. I saw Major Anthony and Major Miller fall, and many of the men.

'My platoon was to attack a tall building on the right. I saw a machine gun firing from an upper window. There was an old cattle shed nearby, so we all dived behind that. Our Bren gunner from behind a stone wall fired up into the window, while Private Andrews ran out and hurled a grenade through the broken glass. End of machine gun!'

Peter lay back and closed his eyes. He seemed to fall asleep but then with renewed vigour continued. 'More firing was coming from what looked like a school house nearby. This was the next for our platoon to capture. It was an ugly situation. I could see the other company was in deep trouble. Many of the men were still lying in the open, killed or wounded. We could do nothing but move on, one section at a time, trying to give covering fire at every step. I somehow knew that something was waiting for me inside that school. We reached the door. I kicked it down. I saw a sudden movement inside, so I threw in a grenade. The explosion inside the hall was deafening. I jumped over two Jerries who had been knocked out, but a burst of fire from a Spandau ripped through my arm and side. That's about all I can remember.'

Peter lay back on his pillow looking exhausted but evidently relieved that his story had been told. A short while later two nurses came and lifted him onto a stretcher and out of the ward, saying that he needed further surgical treatment. He did not come back and his bed was soon reoccupied by a man with a head injury. To my great regret, I did not see Peter again and was unable to find out what became of him.

It was not until after the war that I learnt what happened next.

After the dust from the grenade had subsided, the platoon sergeant rushed to Peter's aid. With another man, he cut away the sleeve from his shattered arm and applied a field dressing. The German who had fired the Spandau was quickly overcome, and the building cleared of the enemy. Soon after, stretcher bearers arrived, attended to the wounded and began the long carry back to the Regimental Aid Post.

By the time that darkness fell the battalion of Grenadier Guards had successfully overcome all resistance at the cinema, schoolhouse, block of flats and the main tower, but at great cost. The Commanding Officer, Lieut-Colonel Gordon Lennox, made sure that all the wounded had been evacuated, and then organised all-round defence, while patrols were sent out to clear the immediate area.

For some hours there was silence. Then shortly before midnight, the German artillery opened up with a shattering barrage. Tracer bullets flashed across the sky, to be answered by fierce machine gun fire from the Guards Brigade. This was the beginning of the battle that we had heard as we waited in our water-logged slit trenches. Then came the violent thunderstorm. It seemed like a fierce war between the gods and men. Following the artillery, the Germans launched the expected counter-attack upon the area of the Factory. The Guards were ready and poured forth a hail of fire into the darkness. During the torrential storm it was impossible to see the enemy. The German infantry stumbled on firing wildly but unable to reach their objectives. Far into the night the battle continued. By first light the Germans had managed to infiltrate back into a cluster of huts about two hundred yards beyond the Factory. As these huts were in a commanding position on high ground, it was essential to drive the enemy out. Colonel Gordon-Lennox could see from the top of the tower that the German infantry were forming up for attack. He ordered No 3 Company to seize the initiative and attack first.

The assault platoon under Lieut. Wedderburn charged across the open ground, while the other platoons gave intensive covering fire. Several of his men fell before reaching their objective, but the Germans were quickly overwhelmed after fierce hand to hand fighting. With only eight men left standing Wedderburn arranged the defence of the huts area, while a team of stretcher bearers ran up to rescue the wounded on both sides.

Towards mid-morning a new crisis arose. The Germans were approaching not only with a company of infantry but with a squadron of tanks. With no anti-tank weapons, Lieut. Wedderburn and his few men were forced to withdraw.

Colonel Gordon-Lennox quickly called for Captain Hohler of No 3 Company and ordered him to attack at once before the tanks could get established and pulverise the factory with shell fire.

Captain Hohler hurried back to his Company where an appalling sight awaited him. A shell had landed in the very room where wounded Guardsmen were being treated. One soldier who had been blinded now lay with both legs blown off. Another guardsman had also lost both legs and several other wounded lay around, including the Company Sergeant Major.

Having ensured that they were being looked after, Captain Hohler organised the attack without delay. The superb discipline and determination of the Guards never wavered. They followed the brave captain in another charge across the open ground, while intense covering fire was given by the other Company. Five men were killed before reaching their objective, but the Germans were ill-prepared for the ferocity of the Guards' charge. The tanks reversed and withdrew, firing tracer bullets as they went.

It was a depleted Company that finally re-occupied the wooden buildings. As Captain Hohler was badly wounded in the arm, Lieut. Wedderburn organised the defences. Within minutes, the deep whirring sound of tank engines warned them that the enemy was not giving up. Suddenly they saw the turret of a German tank only a few feet outside the hut window, while several German soldiers charged inside. Captain Hohler threw himself down as though dead. The Germans seized the hut, ignoring him, but rounding up the few remaining Guardsmen. Eventually Captain Hohler, although faint from loss of blood, managed to crawl back to the Factory, to report that Lieut. Wedderburn and all his platoon were either killed or captured.

Meanwhile another platoon of No 2 Company had been attacked by the tanks while they held the upper storey of a farmhouse. The gunfire of the tanks had blown up the staircase, leaving the men uninjured but unable to withdraw until after dark, when they climbed out of a window and down a drainpipe.

Of the Grenadier Guards Battalion, only No 2 Company remained to make a third attack on the area of the huts. This time they were more fortunate in having the support of American tanks. A fierce tank battle ensued with the Americans dominating with a barrage of shells. The German tanks withdrew, allowing No 2 Company to lay a minefield round the Guards' flank, thus making their position less vulnerable.

While the Grenadiers were fully engaged around the Factory, the Irish Guards had been occupied with their own troubles. After a miserable night, at dawn a short but terrific concentration of enemy shells landed on the battalion position. The Germans had mustered every gun and cannon they could lay their hands on; German, French, Italian, Russian and Yugoslav weapons, modern and obsolete, added to the turmoil. The mud was scattered indescribably, but the Guards as yet suffered remarkably few casualties.

The shelling was followed by three companies of enemy infantry approaching down a disused railway track. At last our own artillery could take revenge. The Germans presented a perfect target. British twenty-five pounders put down a concentration that completely engulfed the advancing German companies. When the smoke lifted not one living German could be seen. Then between lulls in the firing German ambulances appeared to take away the wounded infantry.

But all day long the Irish Guards suffered severely from the shelling. It was impossible to find shelter as every position could clearly be seen from the German observation posts high up in the Alban Hills. During the morning heavy trucks began to arrive with ammunition for the Guards. It was a dangerous journey, clearly visible from the enemy's positions. A shell landed on a lorry of mortar bombs. Instead of exploding all at once the bombs went off spasmodically, wounding the driver of the lorry who was imprisoned in the cab.

Seeing his peril, an Irish orderly-room clerk of Battalion HQ, rushed out of his slit trench and disregarding the danger from the exploding mortar bombs, dragged the driver out of the blazing lorry.

At last the long tragic day drew to a close. Many of the Scots and Irish Guards had been killed or wounded but they had never wavered nor yielded an inch. With the approach of darkness came blessed silence. The artillery fire had been intense and prolonged, directed with merciless accuracy by the Germans on top of the Alban Hills.

The respite was brief, however, for with the dawn the shells crashed down once again. The time had now come for a major offensive to be launched against the enemy, with zero hour to be an hour before midnight. The Scots and Irish Guards were to be the spearhead of the attack, followed by an assault by the Armoured Division on the Alban Hills.

The two Guards Battalions took up their positions on the start-line. The only sound that came through the darkness was the croaking of frogs, until suddenly the shattering roar of the artillery barrage awoke the night, followed immediately by the explosion of shells on the enemy's position.

The Scots and Irish Guards crossed the start-line. The moon had not yet risen so the men had to keep close contact by each man holding the bayonet scabbard of the man in front.

The protection given by the darkness was illusory. The advancing Guards were suddenly illuminated by flares from Very lights, giving the German machine gunners easy targets.

No 2 Company of the Irish Guards drew the first hail of bullets. The leading platoon commander and several men fell dead. The platoon sergeant took over and immediately led his men in a lightning charge on a small house from which tracer was pouring. Using grenades and bayonets they overpowered the Germans, taking several prisoners.

A curtain of steel was still coming from other machine guns sited in a ditch. This deadly fire was partly overcome by one man. Lance-Corporal M.T. O'Brian crawled forward with his two-inch mortar until he could see the muzzle flashes of the guns. It was like crawling towards death itself, but perhaps because of the tendency to fire high at night, the bullets passed over his head. Then setting up his mortar he fired his bombs at low angle directly at the machine guns. The first gun stopped firing so O'Brian turned his mortar towards the next until there was a gap in the enemy lines.

But as the company advanced through the gap, the sound of enemy tanks came from the road. At the same time the moon came from behind a cloud, making the Guards a perfect target for the tanks. Once again it was two individual soldiers who saved the whole company. Two Bren gunners, Taylor and Montgomery, crept towards the tanks. At short range they fired at the tanks' turrets, thus forcing the crews to close their visors. With their field of vision restricted the tanks could no longer fire accurately and the Guardsmen were enabled to run to defensive positions in a deep ditch.

With the enemy all around, the company was isolated. Its only wireless set had been damaged by shell fire. Until it could be repaired the company was out of contact with the rest of the battalion. Lance Corporal Holwell started to work on the set by the light of a shaded torch. As any glimmer might bring down enemy fire upon himself, his work called for the greatest courage and coolness. While shells crashed all around he took the set to pieces. Within a few hours his work was to bring about the saving of both his own and No 1 Company.

Back at Battalion HQ, Colonel Montagu-Douglas-Smith realised that the attack was being opposed far more strongly than expected. The German artillery was firing rapidly with every gun available. Four lorries bringing up ammunition were hit. Huge sheets of flame leapt up as they exploded.

As first light began to appear over the battlefield, the fighting was still continuing all along the front. A message reached HQ from the forward company of the Scots Guards: 'We are surrounded and look like being over-run.' A short while later the company commander was killed and the rest of his company were either casualties or taken prisoner.

The battle had now reached a critical stage. The fate of the two Irish Guards companies was still unknown, until suddenly a voice was heard on Battalion HQ Wireless. No 2 Company was back on the air. After several hours work Corporal Holwell had repaired the damaged set and the two companies were in touch at last. After assessing the scanty information, the Brigadier realised that the Germans had effectively encircled the Irish Battalion. He ordered them to withdraw and fight their way back through the one narrow gap.

The two company commanders made a hurried plan. They would have to fight by leaps and bounds along the line of the railway. The growing number of wounded men presented a problem as it was impossible to evacuate them. A medical orderly, Lance Corporal Moriarti, volunteered to remain with them. He had already spent the night looking for casualties and bringing them to the only place of shelter, a railway bridge over a sunken road. Here they remained all day until they were eventually rescued that night.

Major Stewart-Richardson led the way to cut through the German ring, while Major Fitzgerald remained with his company to give covering fire. As they made a dash for the embankment enemy machine guns fired a stream of bullets at them. Amongst those who fell dead was Lance Corporal Holwell whose calm bravery in repairing his wireless set had saved the companies from complete destruction.

Having reached the embankment they next had to fight their way down the exposed railway line. Two Bren gunners took up positions on the edge of the embankment. Although their heads presented a clear target, they opened fire on the nearest German posts. The first platoon then began its hazardous dash through the enemy's encircling ring; every man must have realised that his chance of surviving was small.

The first platoon commander was killed almost immediately. The platoon split up into small groups, and by a series of dashes, some of them managed to reach the comparative safety of a ditch.

The other platoons then started off on a nightmare charge. The next platoon commander was also killed before he had run a few yards. Major Stewart-Richardson following next, was wounded in the forehead, but managed to lead the scattered groups of men who still survived. With magnificent courage these tall Guardsmen charged down the railway line, jumping over bodies of men killed the night before, almost lost in a hail of bullets, shells and mortar bombs. Inspired by the frenzy of battle, they hurled themselves against the enemy posts, driving them back. More than half of the two gallant companies failed to return, but those who came through owed much to the leadership of the company commanders and to Guardsmen Taylor and Montgomery. Without the covering fire from their Bren Guns the casualties would have been much higher. Taylor had been wounded in the leg but managed to crawl back with his gun intact. The last two men to return were Major Fitzgerald and Guardsman Montgomery, the latter with his Bren Gun blazing to the last.

At mid-day General Penney arrived at Brigade HQ. At about the same time reports came from the remaining companies of the Scots Guards. With the support of American tank destroyers they had systematically attacked and overcome the enemy on the left flank. Any remaining enemy infantry had been cleared or rounded up. With the left flank open the General decided that the way was clear for the delayed attack by the 3rd Brigade to begin.

After their long and anxious wait on the start-line, the Duke of Wellingtons and the Kings Shropshire Light Infantry advanced through the newly captured positions. The tide of war rolled onwards, leaving the Guards to recover from their long ordeal.

So ended one phase in the epic battle of the Guards Brigade. Inspite of tragic losses, they had once again proved themselves to be amongst the finest fighting soldiers in the world.

4
Horror Farm

The night of the violent thunderstorm and the inferno of battle gave way at last to a watery dawn. The countryside was sodden, with trees dripping onto mud and flooded pools. The thunder had gradually rumbled away as though angry at being rivalled by the artillery fire.

By the time the sun rose from behind black clouds, we were already on the march, moving on in the direction of Rome and approaching the sounds of a renewed battle which had flared up at first light. The prospect was not encoraging; we were numb with lack of sleep, while our wet clothes clung to shivering bodies. As we marched we were kept going by the sound of bagpipes, one piper having been allotted to each company. In our generally miserable circumstances it was indeed remarkable how the steady rhythm and shrill, elemental sound of the pipes enlivened the spirit and inspired courage when most needed.

For a while the sounds of battle ceased, as though the enemy was waiting silently for us to draw near. We tramped on, passing the Factory, so recently captured by the Grenadier Guards, many of the buildings being scarred by shell and mortar fire. It now lay deserted as it remained a prime target for the German artillery on the Alban Hills. The Grenadiers had meanwhile taken up more secure positions on the left of the disused railway line.

About a mile north of the Factory, Colonel Peddie established his HQ near a horribly smelly farm, already named Dung Farm. Piles of manure beside cattle sheds remained, all the animals and farm workers having vanished. (The HQ was mercifully up-wind!) We marched on beyond the smells until we were given positions on the crest of a long northward stretching ridge, later to be known as the Thumb. Our company was on the right of the Battalion, while D, A, and C Companies were further along on the left.

Our first duty was to select new positions facing the enemy – or rather where the enemy were thought to be. While the men dug trenches which quickly became waterlogged, I took three men with me to gather any information about the enemy on the right side of our ridge. Sporadic gunfire was still coming from the direction of the Guards Brigade, and it was essential for us to ascertain any enemy movements on the right flank.

6TH GORDONS AT HORROR FARM

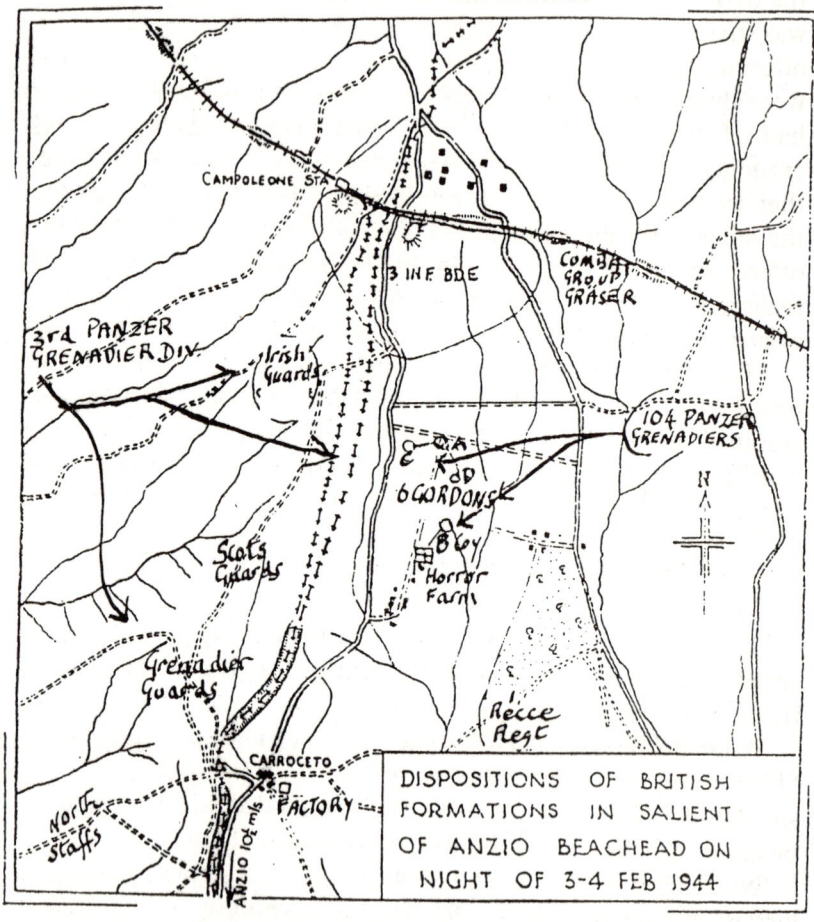

Map: Dispositions of British formations in salient of Anzio beachead on night of 3-4 Feb 1944. Labels include Campoleone Sta, 3rd Panzer Grenadier Div, 3 Inf Bde, Combat Group Graser, Irish Guards, 104 Panzer Grenadiers, Scots Guards, 6 Gordons, Horror Farm, Grenadier Guards, Recce Regt, Carroceto, Factory, North Staffs, Anzio 10½ mls.

The flat countryside seemed deserted. Only a criss-crossing of tank tracks had left the mud churned up as the tanks had moved on the day before in support of the beleaguered Scots Guards. But now there was no sign of the enemy, or indeed any form of life. What had been good farmland was now deserted even by birds. For several miles we searched and listened, moving carefully, avoiding any bare areas where we might easily be seen.

Then unexpectedly we came upon a small cottage beside a barn, half hidden behind a group of trees. Seeing a wisp of smoke rising from a chimney we banged on the door. After a long pause, a wizened old man opened, looking terrified at our rifles. He waved us away and tried to shut the door, but we took the precaution of looking inside the dark interior where an old woman, shrivelled into a ball of rags, was stirring some mixture in a pot. We tried to alleviate their fear by offering them a bar of chocolate. By signs we ascertained that they were alone, their nearest neighbours having moved away. They still had a few hens and a goat in milk which evidently provided a bare existence. It seemed useless for us to try to warn them of the danger they were in. Their isolated cottage no doubt seemed far away from the noise of warfare, which was of no concern to them. When they offered us a handful of eggs as a bribe to leave them unmolested, we realised we could do nothing to help and so left them to their lonely existence, hoping the tide of war would pass them by.

After completing a wide sweep of the area, we returned to base. I hurried to Company HQ and jumped down into Major Bridgman's cramped slit trench. He looked tired and anxious but had not lost his usual good humour. 'You've been a long time, Ted,' he remarked. 'Got as far as Rome?'

'Not quite,' I replied. 'We went for afternoon tea with an Italian farmer and his wife.'

'You greedy lot! Why was I not invited?'

'The truth of the matter is that they were an ancient and infirm couple left behind on their own, they thought we were going to shoot them.' I described their bleak circumstances.

Major Bridgman reflected a few moments and then commented, 'They were right to stay. Rather than be uprooted at that age, they should, if it had to be, die together in their own home. Now to business. You saw no signs of the Germans?'

'Nothing at all. But in the north we heard distant rumblings of lorries and perhaps tanks. It sounded as though a large enemy formation was on the move.'

'You're probably right. I've just come back from Battalion HQ.' He opened his map. 'Colonel Peddie warns us we may be the spearhead of a new attack at dawn tomorrow. Much depends on how soon the Guards Brigade can drive the Germans out of Campoleone Station – there, where the two disused railway lines cross. Yesterday the Irish Guards fought a very fierce battle on the left of the railway.

Now the Scots and the Irish are both in the thick of it. It sounds as though they've been fighting all day, God help them. The task of our Brigade will be to start a big offensive beyond Campoleone, once the Germans have been driven out. At the same time an American armoured Brigade will storm up the Alban Hills.'

'That seems the most urgent of all, – to get rid of that pestilent artillery shooting us up all the time.'

'You're right. Better go and tell the General. Meanwhile you should go and try to get some rest. Be ready for dawn tomorrow. Patrols are being sent out through the night by A and D Companies. You've done your turn.'

At dawn the next morning we were still waiting. No order to advance came. The hours passed. About noon a message reached us from Battalion HQ that the time for attack had been postponed. The Guards had finally triumphed after suffering heavy losses, but it had taken a day longer than planned. The 3rd Brigade, with the Duke of Wellingtons and the KSLI, were even now passing through the Guards positions and attacking the Germans.

For the next twenty-four hours we remained shivering in our wet slit trenches. The shelling from the Germans on the Alban Hills continued relentlessly. Dung Farm with its prominent buildings was a favourite target, the shells landing perilously near Battalion HQ. Only a few stray shells exploded near our company, but they were enough to make life unpleasant, as we knew that any movement would be seen and fired on by the German gunners.

So the miserable day dragged on. The sounds of battle sounded all around us, but the fog of war had descended, preventing any clear understanding of the situation. During a lull in the firing I went to see Lindsay Bridgman. 'When are we going to move on?' I asked. 'The Jocks are getting browned off.'

Lindsay nodded. 'Aren't we all? It seems that things have changed today. Colonel Peddie tells me that our planned offensive has been postponed. The General now intends to hold all our present positions against an enemy counter-attack which is expected any time. We're in a vital position on this ridge as we guard the right flank. General Penney warns that unless we hold out here the entire flank of the First Division might collapse.'

'Sounds like a story from the Boys' Own Paper.' I suggested.

'I wish it were. Our other three companies are in an equally exposed position. The CO was in an unusually grim mood this morning. Didn't even smile at me.'

'Breach of King's Regulations: Failing to smile at one company commander.'

'Yes, well, I'm not in a smiling mood myself today. Anyway, you've bought yourself another patrol tonight. Three men as usual. Got your map ready? These three farms here, then in a wide circle to watch and listen. Report any signs or sounds of the enemy. Remember the indications are that a whole fresh German division is on its way to surround us.'

However many times I went on night patrol, the prospects were always daunting. During the hours before departure I felt an ache in the pit of my stomach. Although the time was spent in preparation and memorising the route on the map, the fear of the unknown cast its gloom however one tried to make light of it. On this occasion I took with me Corporal Allardice, McKinnel and Forbes, all hardened scouts.

The night was very dark with low clouds and a light rain falling. We went cautiously down the slope of the ridge, and across open country. Frequently we stumbled against unseen obstacles. Black shapes which might have been anything, sometimes seemed to move and then disappear. Eventually, thanks to frequent compass readings, we found the three farms. Each one appeared to be deserted. As we stood and listened we heard the unmistakable rumbling of heavy vehicles and perhaps tanks coming from a northerly direction. It sounded as though they were moving slowly, perhaps to keep the noise of their engines to a minimum.

Nothing more was to be seen, so with this information we hurried back, again carefully checking our compass bearings. It was two in the morning by the time I reported to Major Bridgman.

'Come back and see me in an hour.' he said, 'Messages are coming through on the wireless. I may have more for you.'

I returned to my platoon and made sure everyone was alert and well prepared.

An hour later I stood with Major Bridgman trying to see into the darkness. All the guns on every sector were now quite silent; somehow the silence was more ominous than the usual background noise of artillery fire.

Suddenly looking in the direction of Rome, I saw a jagged line of flames flash up into the darkness. With equal rapidity Major Bridgman and I dived into our trenches. Two seconds of complete silence. Then a shriek in the air above us and a tremendous explosion which seemed only a few yards away. For the next twenty minutes an intense bombardment rained down upon us. Shells exploded in an ear-shattering cacophony. One could do nothing but crouch down as far as possible into the slit trench, listening to the spiteful hiss and crash of each shell, and praying that none would land on top of one's head.

When at last the barrage suddenly ceased, my ears were ringing. When I shouted, 'Are you OK Sergeant Maclaren?' I could hardly hear my own voice or his reply, 'OK sir.'

I jumped out of my trench and ran across the shell-pitted ground to see the section positions.

'OK Corporal Tripney?'

'One man knocked out by shrapnel, sir. Not badly injured.'

'Stand by for the Jerries' attack. Don't fire till they're on you.'

In the other sections two men were wounded, but the application of field dressings was all that could be done for them at that time. It was amazing how near some of the shells had landed without smashing the narrow trenches – in one case a crater was only three feet away from the edge; the men were covered with a shower of mud and earth, but uninjured.

The unnatural silence lasted less than a minute. We knew the barrage must have been the prelude to an attack, but could never have imagined the intensity of machine gun fire which suddenly shattered the darkness. From both our flanks bullets flashed over our heads with the fierceness of a great hailstorm. They hit the ground all around, some ricocheting and flying on in every direction. Tracer bullets split the air like sparks from a volcano.

As yet we could not see the enemy, so we did not give away our positions by uselessly firing back. Behind us from the direction of Battalion HQ came the unmistakable sound of British Bren guns firing repeated steady bursts. If the main enemy attack was starting in our rear we should not be in a happy position, for there was a danger that we might be completely surrounded.

The night was very dark; although I could see nothing I suddenly heard the near-at-hand Bren and rifle fire coming from Corporal Tripney's section. As they ceased, the sounds of shouts and groaning came from the darkness in front. A voice wailed into the night: 'Otto, Otto! Ich sterbe! Otto hilfe!'

But Otto never came to answer his cry for help. Soon the groans grew fainter and were heard no more.

For some hours the firing continued. The Brens near Battalion HQ (probably belonging to our Carrier Platoon) were still firing. Fierce fighting also sounded all around our other three companies further along the ridge.

Soon I realised that the high ground in front of us was already occupied by the enemy. Bursts of machine gun fire passed over our slit trenches from a very short range, and I could hear German voices giving out hasty orders.

Then the first attack came. After a salvo of mortar fire erupted just in front of us, followed by bursts from machine guns, we could just see the black outlines of men looming up in open order. My section commanders perfectly fulfilled their orders not to fire too soon. When the enemy were near enough to present a perfect target, I yelled 'FIRE!' With all our weapons discharging at once the effect was startling. The black shapes disappeared as though they had never been. More shouts and cries for help followed; some injured men were evidently being carried or dragged back. While the enemy tried to reorganise we remained silent, hoping that the enemy would over-estimate our strength.

Suddenly the almost ghostlike figure of Mennim, our Company runner, jumped into the trench beside me. 'Major Bridgman wants to see you, sir.'

We both climbed out of the trench, and half crawled, half ran across the open stretch of ground to Company HQ. I lay down behind the slight protection of the earth round Lindsay Bridgman's trench.

'Good show, Ted,' he whispered. 'Must have been a German fighting patrol. You taught them a lesson.'

'They'll come again, with more fire power next time.'

Another figure crouched down beside me in the darkness.

'Is that you Norman?' Bridgman asked. 'You all right?'

'Yes, all except Sergeant Thain. He's killed. He was wonderful – firing our captured machine gun as the Jerries charged. He took no notice of the enemy fire until he was shot through the heart.'

'God help him!'

'He stopped their attack. But they're starting to dig in only a short distance in front of us. Corporal Agnew crawled forward and chucked some grenades at them, so they started digging again a bit further away.'

'The ridge in front of my platoon is occupied now too,' I added. 'I can't say yet how many.'

Major Bridgman grunted. 'A wireless message has come from the CO ordering us to attack at dawn to drive them right off the hill. We can get no support. The other three companies are completely out of touch.'

'Is Battalion HQ still intact?'

'Yes, but they're having a rough time. It must be Robin Bain and his Carriers who are driving back the attacks. Well I can't give any orders yet. It's now half past three. Come back here in an hour if you can.'

Norman and I crawled away into the darkness to visit our section commanders. I had evidently moved nearer to the enemy than I realised for the sounds of Germans digging were unmistakable. As I strained my ears listening it seemed as though a large number of picks and shovels were being plied only a very short distance in front of us. Suddenly I heard a German voice louder than the other noises. It sounded as though an officer was attempting to make himself heard on the wireless.

Twice he repeated in German, 'Yes, my Company is in position here, beside No 1 Company. Two more companies are behind us.'

The significance of this message hit me with stunning realisation: my platoon, now with about twenty-five men, was opposed by two German companies of two hundred men each, and two more companies behind them!

I called for Wilson, my platoon runner. 'Go and tell Major Bridgman that we have two whole companies of Jerries in front of us digging in. I'll come and see him myself soon.'

After waiting a short while in the hope of hearing more, I ran across the muddy ground to confirm my message to Lindsay Bridgman.

'What's all this?' he demanded as I crouched down beside his slit trench.

'Two companies in position just in front of my platoon. Two more behind. I heard a German officer reporting this over his wireless.'

'Well, I've sent the information back to Battalion HQ. But I don't think they'll be able to help us. We're more or less surrounded.'

Lindsay Bridgman was speaking quietly and casually as though this were an everyday occurrence, but we both realised that the situation was critical. After a pause he added, 'So whatever happens we'll have to fight our way out.'

Once more I crawled back to warn my platoon to hold on all night and be ready to attack at dawn. The sounds of battle on our left had now changed. The earlier conflagration involving our other three companies had ceased. Behind us the unmistakable steady zut-zut-zut of our Bren guns (about three rounds a second) and the fast shower of bullets from German Spandaus, indicated that the exchange of fire around Battalion HQ was still continuing.

As we waited anxiously through the dark hours of the night, we heard the continual blows of pick and shovel in front of us. We could envisage the strong force of the enemy waiting for us, with well sited machine guns and hundreds of men in their newly dug trenches. It would need a miracle if we were to fight our way through such a waiting wall of fire.

Shortly before five o'clock a new outburst of firing came from the direction of Norman's platoon. This was followed by the arrival of Mennim to fetch me again to see Major Bridgman. Norman and I reached Company HQ together.

'The CO's orders have just been confirmed,' said Major Bridgman in a toneless voice. 'There's nothing left for us to do but drive the enemy off this ridge. Each platoon will attack the enemy positions at first light.'

'My platoon's completely pinned down.' said Norman. 'The Jerries have brought up machine guns and started firing at us from close range.'

'Very well, Ted will have to make the attack while you will give all the covering fire you can.'

At this moment the signaller on the 18 wireless set handed Major Bridgman the earphones. 'Message coming through sir.'

We waited tensely while Major Bridgman listened. The news could hardly be worse than it was at that moment.

'Postpone present orders.' announced the Major at length. 'We may be getting tanks to help us. Thank God for that! There's hope for us once again.'

'When will the tanks arrive?'

'There's nothing definite yet. No news from the other companies for several hours. They just seem to have vanished into the night.'

For some minutes which seemed hours we waited in silence, hoping against hope that the tanks would materialise. In the east the blackness of night was already showing a pale gleam.

'In half an hour we shall have to attack whether the tanks come or not.' Major Bridgman peered into the sky as though trying to delay the coming of dawn. His voice gave no hint that he knew as well as we did how hopeless would be our task without the support of tanks.

The light was now unmistakably growing. The few sparse bushes in front of us looked like crouching men. They even swayed and seemed to move towards us as the dawn wind increased. Unless the message came soon Norman and I would have the greatest difficulty in returning across the open ground to our platoons. There in the gathering light the enemy was silently waiting. If we delayed too long they would attack first.

Major Bridgman looked at his luminous watch and again at the sky. 'We can't wait any longer. You'd both better get back now. Norman fire like Hell and keep the Jerries' heads down. Ted will start the attack in eleven minutes from now. Good Luck!'

Just as we were cautiously rising to dash back to our platoons the signaller again waved the earphones. We waited for the message on which our very lives depended.

In the dim light we watched Major Bridgman put on the earphones. A slight smile came to his eyes as he nodded, 'Roger Out!' He looked up at us. 'Five Sherman tanks are on their way! Here in fifteen minutes. We're to follow them up, clear the enemy from their trenches and round up the prisoners.'

'Sounds easy,' muttered Norman, 'What if the Germans don't like the idea? They may have plans of their own, such as Tiger tanks.'

'It's who gets there first. Get cracking!'

Norman and I rushed back to give out the new orders. Just as he dived into his trench, the machine gun opposite opened up with angry bursts. From the distance along the ridge came the ominous sound of tanks revving up.

Ten minutes later the ground shook and from behind us we heard tanks approaching at top speed. The leading Sherman burst out of the thick shrubs but at the same moment machine guns and rifle fire shattered the air above us. This was the moment the Gemans had planned. The two attacks were beginning so simultaneously that one might have thought a referee had blown a whistle for the battle to begin. The appearance of the Sherman must have caused great alarm, for the Germans fired off every weapon in continuous bursts. A shell landed just beside a tank which rumbled onwards in a scornful manner.

Then a tremendous bang sounded above my head. Another tank

was just behind my trench, its 75mm gun slightly smoking. Some two hundred yards away a German anti-tank gun (which had evidently fired at the leading Sherman) was completely destroyed together with the tree that had camouflaged it.

With added confidence the two tanks slowly advanced on the enemy, while three more approached from behind. Thundering right up to the enemy trenches they poured a hail of machine gun bullets on top of the helpless Germans. From other trenches numbers of the enemy jumped and began running down the hill.

This was our great opportunity and we opened up with all we had. As our Bren guns rattled I saw Corporal Moir climb out of his trench completely exposed to enemy bullets to direct the fire. Now the red-headed Gourlay stood up in the open firing round after round from his rifle.

Calling to Corporal Boyes to follow I made a dash to a ditch not far in front. Several dead Germans were lying in this but we had no time to notice them. From here we had a good field of fire looking down on some of the newly dug German trenches. After firing a magazine, my Tommy Gun jammed. Before trying to adjust it I noticed one of the dead Germans had been carrying a British Bren gun. Quickly grabbing it I found it fired perfectly.

After their initial shock the Germans reorganised remarkably swiftly. The platoons behind moved forward and fired showers of bullets at the tank turrets and towards us infantry. Now the moment had arrived for us to put into practice all our training for combined operations with tanks. So shouting to my platoon we all rushed behind the two leading tanks which began to move forward again. In leaps and bounds we followed the tanks. While they fired downwards into the terrified Germans we rounded up all those who tried to put up any resistance, or who put up their hands in surrender.

The battlefield was in a turmoil of fire and crossfire. Although our tanks dominated the enemy, there were still many Germans in protected positions some distance away who poured a steady stream of machine gun fire into the maelstrom. The tanks were magnificent: the commander of the leading Sherman seemed to have an uncanny gift of spotting camouflaged anti-tank guns and knocking it out before it could fire. He continued to risk his own life by standing unprotected in his turret directing fire.

So on we went; first the tanks, then we would rush from their protective flanks to take as many prisoners as we could round up or force to surrender. As we had heard during the night, trenches had been dug everywhere. In some we found Germans lying dead, in others the enemy quickly jumped out when they saw our bayonets prodding them from above. From further back machine guns were still firing, but soon became confused so that the bullets found no precise targets and flew around haphazardly.

As we cleared the trenches, we herded all the prisoners into a hollow. An officer from one of the Shermans waved his arm to me, shouting 'Tiger tanks!' Immediately the other tanks swirled round and moved on to meet this new threat.

By now over a hundred prisoners were huddled together in the hollow. 'Get moving!' I shouted to them in German, 'We'll all be shelled!' This threat spurred them on. After a hasty search for hidden weapons, we marched them back towards our own lines. Amongst those captured were four officers, one of them a captain.

'Do these men belong to your company?' I asked him.

'Jawohl,' he answered proudly, 'they are all good soldiers of No 2 Company. Those men behind are from No 1 Company.'

So it had been his voice that I had heard speaking over the wireless giving us this vital information!

'What were your orders last night when you dug in here?'

'I'm not obliged to answer. My name is Schneider – Captain Otto Schneider. I say no more.' He was a tall, well built man who, although being taken prisoner, had not lost his dignity. More machine gun fire flashed overhead, so I detailed four men to escort the prisoners back to Battalion HQ. With the rest of the platoon I searched the area in case more Germans had been left behind.

We were now on a slight rise overlooking the surrounding country. In the grey light of the early morning, I saw the dim outline of enemy tanks slowly approaching; one, two, four, now six tanks were clearly visible. At first they seemed to be heading straight towards us. Then at some signal from the leader they veered south-westwards directly towards the positions held by our A, C and D Companies.

'God help them!' I cried. 'They'll be completely overrun!'

Although the battlefield around these companies had been strangely quiet during the night, the forward companies now opened up with a shattering outburst of all their weapons, but they could do little against the power of the tanks which as they moved forward gave each other fierce covering fire.

Then over a rise I saw a wave of enemy infantry following behind the tanks. Firing as they ran, they began a ferocious assault on our companies.

Before I could do anything, a shout came from Corporal Boyes. 'Watch out, sir! More tanks coming this way!'

A burst of machine gun fire reinforced his words. The only way we could help our three beleaguered companies was to let Battalion HQ know what was happening. We rushed back to where Major Bridgman was anxiously waiting.

'Our wireless has been knocked out by a shell,' he said when I stressed the urgency. 'All I can do is to send a runner with a message.' This he did without delay. Several hours later the runner had not returned. What became of him we never knew – probably hit by one of the many shells. In the heat of the battle the vital message presumably never arrived.

Meanwhile a tank battle was at its height. About half a mile away our five Shermans were in hull-down positions firing over the brow of a slight hill. We could see two Tiger tanks advancing to our left flank, evidently intending to shoot the Shermans from the side.

From the direction of the three companies came the unmistakable sound of Brens and rifles, all merged into the horrifying tumult of two armies clashing in mortal conflict. A, C and D Companies were fighting back in a desperate attempt to save themselves.

From our own Company HQ, now mercifully no longer in the direct firing line, Major Bridgman and I exchanged woeful glances. We both knew that infantry alone, with no other support, could have no chance against German Tiger tanks supporting each other and followed by hoards of infantry. Suddenly one of the Tiger tanks gave a shudder and began pouring forth black smoke. We gave a cheer for the Sherman which had hit the Tiger. One of the Shermans then came racing back, evidently to cut off the enemy's advance by a flanking movement. The commander of the Sherman, whom I recognised as the officer who had so bravely headed our attack, was standing in the turret, apparently oblivious of the fact that blood was streaming down his face.

Gradually the battle grew further away on our left. The sound of Bren gun fire had ceased. Soon the whole battlefield became ominously quiet. One could only imagine what must have been the fate of our three gallant companies. I returned to my own platoon position to make sure that the men were digging to strengthen their slit trenches after the pounding from the artillery.

About an hour later, Mennim came to ask me to return to Company HQ. Jimmy Williamson, the adjutant, had just arrived and was talking to Major Bridgman. 'Glad to see you both.' he exclaimed. 'We couldn't get you on the RT.'

'Our 18 set is smashed,' explained Major Bridgman. 'I sent a message with a runner. Didn't you get it?'

'There's so much shelling around HQ anything might have happened. But I got no message.'

'We tried to warn you about the tanks and infantry attacking the three companies.'

'That's why I'm here. No word or message from them for several hours. God knows what's happened.'

'I saw what happened,' I said. 'At least six Tiger tanks pitched right into them firing right down into their trenches. Then at least a battalion of infantry followed behind. I heard them fighting back, their Brens and rifles blazing. But they didn't stand a chance. Our own Shermans were fighting a battle of their own, so couldn't help.'

'I'm going forward to try to find out what's become of them. Meanwhile the CO wants you to hang on here. The enemy may attack again at any moment.' Then turning to me he added, 'Oh and thanks for all the prisoners you sent us!'

With a brief wave, he strode on along the ridge, all alone and armed with nothing but a pistol. He was a tall man, aged about thirty, with a thin, lithe figure. He moved with the easy assurance of a young laird striding over the hills at home. We watched him disappear over the far side of the ridge, and wondered if he would be seen by the machine gunners who still occupied commanding sites a short distance away.

About an hour later, he returned, his legs covered in mud, and brandishing his pistol at eight dejected-looking German soldiers slouching in front of him.

'I've brought a few more prisoners to add to your bag.' he announced. 'But the three companies have completely disappeared. No sign of them whatever. So now the Battalion consists of B Company and HQ – nothing else!'

The three of us looked at each other in grim silence. Then Major Bridgman signed to two men to take charge of the prisoners. 'How on earth did you manage to capture these men all on your own?' he asked.

'I heard some German voices behind a bush,' answered Williamson with a slight smile. 'They might come in useful, I thought, so I went round and caught them.'

How he had achieved this, or had searched the bullet-swept area alone in the face of further enemy attacks at any moment, we never learned. We were still in a critical position, exposed on a long salient with the German division ready to strike before our missing companies could be replaced. Both Norman's and No 11 platoons were still opposed by well sited machine guns which had been protected from the tanks.

During the morning and all afternoon the enemy artillery and mortars intensified their harassing fire. At regular intervals came the horrifying sound of 'Anzio Annie', the huge 280mm shells from the railway-mounted guns hidden in caves in the Alban Hills. These monsters had a range of over thirty miles and could land anywhere on the beach-head and on the shipping out to sea. The sound of one of the shells hurtling through the air was like an aerial express train which completed its journey with a gigantic explosion.

As it grew dusk, bursts of machine gun fire grew more frequent and seemed nearer as though the enemy were infiltrating back again into the trenches facing us. The Shermans had finally driven off the Tiger tanks, but we were warned that they would be too heavily committed elsewhere to help us again.

So ended this harrowing day. Although the enemy had not renewed their attack, we endured many long hours of shells bursting in our midst. Thanks to the protection of our trenches the number of direct casualties were few, but lack of sleep and no proper food, combined with the continual shocks to one's nervous system, did not improve our tempers. Throughout the day it was necessary to fire bursts of Bren gun and mortar fire towards the enemy positions in the hope of making them think our strength was much greater than it really was. The fact that no infantry dared to attack gave us some consolation!

The American military historian, Carlo D'Este, later described the position:*

> The key to the fragile British defence became a single company of beleaguered Irish Guards and the remaining company of the Gordons. Despite being outnumbered and outgunned, they managed to prevent the Germans from isolating and destroying

Fatal Decision p.199 (Harper Collins)

the 3rd Brigade. No 4 Company of the Guards had somehow managed to remain mostly intact and, before withdrawing to Dung Farm, captured over a hundred Germans. To its right B Company of the Gordons clung grimly to its positions throughout the day, and it was this tenacity that kept the entire right flank from collapsing.'

By nightfall it was obvious that we would face a situation even more perilous than the night before. Our B Company, already depleted, was alone on this ridge, the only defender of the salient. On our left, was one, equally depleted, company of the Irish Guards. Behind us the sounds of a new battle was raging. We could only hope that reserve forces were fighting to break through.

At midnight a message came for platoon commanders to see Major Bridgman. With lack of sleep and worry, his face was drawn and pale, but outwardly he remained cheerful. 'Good news at last, chaps,' he greeted us. 'The 1st London Scottish are hoping to break through and take over our positions. In one hour we are to withdraw.' We all remained silent, too relieved to speak. 'I've been to see James Peddie,' he continued. 'It seems that General Penney has been insisting on help for our hard pressed Division, The 168th Brigade has just disembarked at Anzio port and General Penney decided that the London Scottish were the ideal regiment to rescue their fellow Scots.'

'Let's hope that we're not called upon to rescue them,' commented Norman. The noises of battle continued, while flashes from mortars and tracer bullets shattered the darkness.

For two more hours we waited, while the enemy bombarded us continually. The only relatively safe places were at the bottom of our slit trenches. Then a new thunderstorm added its ferocity to the turmoil. Rain fell in torrents forming ponds at the bottom of the trenches.

Mercifully, the artillery ceased by three o'clock in the morning, but by now the farm behind Battalion HQ was in flames. Barns, haystacks and farm buildings were blazing furiously, making a perfect target for the enemy gunners. Then the doctor, Captain MacIntosh, came up in a Bren carrier to take away the last of our wounded. When at last the moment came for us to assemble and march off, the black thunder-clouds provided the darkness we needed to remain unseen. At Battalion HQ the Regimental Sergeant Major was waiting to escort us through the surrounding orchards which formed a screen against the glare from the blazing farm.

The scene was like a fantastic nightmare. This was our Battalion: one company, bedraggled but unbeaten, a few Bren carriers and anti-tank guns, Jeeps carrying ammunition, stretcher bearers silently moving among the wreckage, and finally Battalion HQ. Inspite of the intense shelling, the heart of the Battalion had never faltered. Jimmy Williamson, after his heroic exploit, was still organising; Jimmy Leckie, the Signals officer (who was later killed by a shell) had personally kept communications alive throughout the battle; Jimmy Methven, the Intelligence Officer (later seriously wounded), had fetched and escorted the Sherman tanks to reach us just in time. At the head of it all, James Peddie, the Commanding Officer, had held firm without ever wavering, during the fiercest part of the enemy's attack. As we marched past the farm he was standing there beside the blazing barns waiting until the last man had passed. We saw him giving out orders as calmly as though this had been a peacetime barracks.

The rain was turning the roads and tracks into rivers as we marched away into the darkness, leaving behind the flaming inferno of Horror Farm.

5
Epic Battles

After a five mile march through the deluge we were put into reserve positions on a bleak hillside, where we spent the remainder of the night shivering and digging the inevitable slit trenches. As neither sleep nor rest were possible, we stood with our feet in water while the sounds of battle thundered all around. My thoughts inevitably returned to wonder what exactly had been the fate of the three missing companies. The only witnesses of the beginning of the German tank and infantry attack were Corporal Boyes, myself and a few men of my platoon from the vantage point of the ridge. The few survivors who returned from prison camps after the war told of great confusion, but under the rain of bullets and shells, none of them could give a coherent picture of their final hour. It is quite clear from what we saw and heard that the three companies put up a heroic defence against overwhelming odds. In particular, Major Hutcheon, the A Company commander, tried to warn Colonel Peddie of their predicament. When their wireless was smashed by a shell, he sent Lieutenant Harry Garioch with an urgent message. Garioch counted as many as seventeen enemy tanks approaching their position. But as soon as he started on his dangerous journey to Battalion HQ he was taken prisoner. During an artillery barrage he managed to escape back to his company. Major Hutcheon then decided to go himself, but no sooner had he climbed out of his trench than he was mown down by a burst of machine gun fire.

No message therefore ever reached Colonel Peddie, who in any event would have been powerless to send any reinforcements. Once A Company had been overwhelmed, the flanks of C and D Companies were wide open to the enemy, so they were equally powerless to stem the German onslaught.

Nevertheless the Germans suffered very many casualties in their attack. Many of the Tiger tanks were eventually either knocked out or driven back by the gallant Shermans. The German infantry had received a severe battering from our artillery and from the intense fire from our companies. Indeed, according to a German prisoner they would have been only too glad to have surrendered themselves.

Meanwhile we felt that we were in the eye of the storm. All around, both German and Allied artillery were sending shrieking missiles at each other, and the noise of infantry battles continued throughout the night. Inevitably the men of No 10 platoon, enduring hunger, the rain and biting wind, expected me to let them know what was happening. 'What's the news, sir?' 'What are we here for, sir?' 'Why can't we move on? Anything's better than just standing here like fucking sheep waiting slaughter.'

If only I could have known the answers to their questions! While the whole beach-head was aflame with fighting, it was impossible for the men in the midst to have any idea of the overall picture. Had I known then, I would have realised that the true events were even more alarming than could have been imagined.

Two events, in particular, which were revealed later, were on an unforgettable epic scale. The first was the solo battle fought by Major W P Sidney (later Lord De L'Isle and Dudley, a descendant of the Elizabethan Sir Philip Sidney) of the Grenadier Guards. At the beginning of the German offensive to capture the town of Carroceto and the Factory, the hard pressed Guards Brigade were up against the 1st German Parachute Corps and the 65th Infantry Division, supported by tanks. The attack began just before midnight, the main thrust being against the Guards whose last defence line was along a gulley thick with thorny brambles. There was, however, a gap in these thorns used by the Italians as a passage for sheep. As the German infantry began to charge yelling towards this vital gap, Major Sidney with two other Guardsmen rushed to oppose them. Like Horatius of old

> Straight against the great array
> Forth went the dauntless three.

Armed only with a Tommy gun he faced an entire German Battalion. As the enemy charged through the gap he poured forth a hail of bullets until his gun jammed. Then as the two Guardsmen primed grenades he hurled them into the oncoming enemy. One Guardsman was killed and Major Sidney wounded in the leg, but still he kept on throwing grenades until an enemy grenade hit him in the face. Even then he remained defending the gap. Eventually he was relieved by a unit of American parachutists, by which time the German onslaught had been repulsed.

Major Sidney, having recovered from his wounds, was later awarded the VC which was presented to him in the field by a fellow Guardsman, Lord Alexander.

Even today it might be sung of Major Sidney:

> Still is the story told,
> How well Horatius kept the bridge
> In the brave days of old.*

The second epic battle was fought by the Darby Rangers in a valiant but tragic attempt to capture Cisterna, the town which was the main obstacle to our advance to the Alban Hills. In some way the attack was reminiscent of the Charge of the Light Brigade, not because of a wrong order, but because the town which had been only lightly defended was transformed over night by the Germans into a fearsome fortress which the gallant Americans had to attack. They were quickly engulfed in a Hell of firepower from which there was no escape.

The original plan of General Truscott was simple; a three-pronged attack by the US 3rd Division, the 504 Parachute Division and the Darby Rangers. Colonel Darby envisaged a way to capture the town by sending the 1st and 3rd Battalions of his specially trained Rangers by night up a deep trench named the Pantano Ditch. This would bring them within a mile of the town which they could infiltrate before dawn and throw the defenders into confusion, while the 4th Ranger Battalion with the infantry made the main attack.

At one o'clock in the morning the Rangers climbed down in single file into the deep trench. Each man was armed with bandoliers of bullets and pockets bulging with grenades. Silently as they crept forward they had to freeze every time German sentries marched along the sides of the ditch. The darkness of the night fortunately hid them from the enemy. Progess was slow as the two battalions were spread out in a snake-like column. When the leading battalion was still over half a mile from the town, they became aware of the first glimmer of dawn. The ditch came to an end where it met the road to Cisterna so they were obliged to march along this road as the light quickly revealed their presence.

As they neared the town, the whole countryside awoke with a shattering crash. The Rangers were marching straight into an ambush.

Lays of Ancient Rome – Thomas Babington Macaulay

U.S. DARBY RANGERS BATTLE FOR CISTERNA

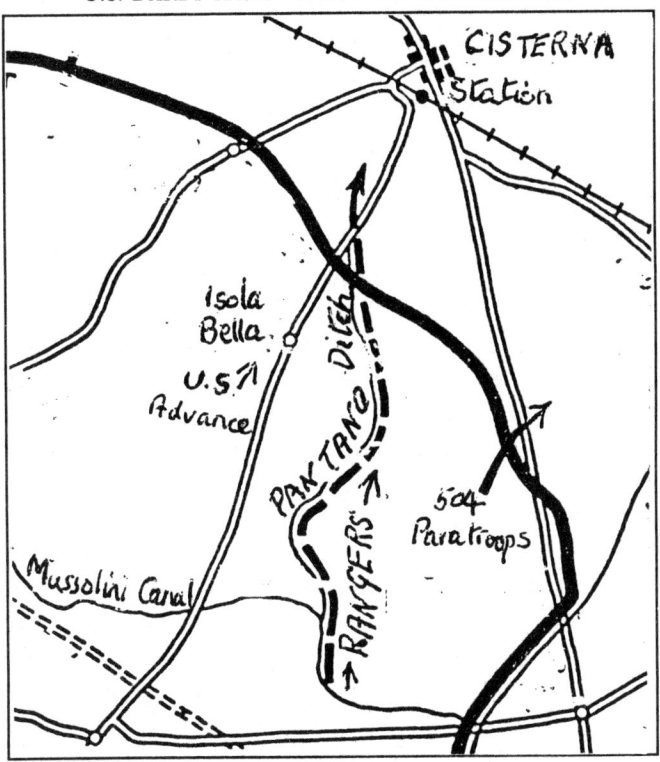

[Map showing: Cisterna Station, Isola Bella, U.S 71 Advance, Pantano Ditch, Rangers, 504 Paratroops, Mussolini Canal]

Three self-propelled guns and machine guns opened heavy fire from hidden positions behind buildings and haystacks.

The Rangers rushed off the road, and in a swift deploying movement manged to knock out all three of the guns with bazookas. But German machine guns poured a torrent of fire from behind protective buildings. As the daylight grew, the men were caught mercilessly without cover or protection. In spite of this, the Rangers never wavered nor gave up their determination to attack at all costs. Some managed to scramble into ditches from where they opened fire on the enemy. Others braved the bullets and reached some of the buildings on the outskirts of the town. But it was a hopeless task from which they did not return.

Meanwhile the 4th Ranger Battalion were advancing up the road, which according to intelligence reports should have been clear of enemy. But now the whole area was strongly defended by newly arrived troops of the Hermann Goering Division with a machine gun battalion and part of the 26th Panzer Division.

As soon as his men came under fire, the American commander attempted an attack on the Germans with two tank destroyers as the spearhead. But these ran straight into a minefield and the attack was held up only 200 yards from the enemy positions.

The 4th Rangers were thus pinned down by an array of well sited machine guns and could do nothing to help their compatriots in their desperate plight.

At noon their last hope faded. Instead of the planned Rangers' attack, German tanks raced down the road towards them, driving right through the Americans' position in the open fields and in the ditches alongside the road. The tanks shot down into the ditches and onto the men in the open. It was a terrible slaughter. But still the Rangers fought back and fired their bazookas at the tanks. One was quickly in flames. A second was hit with a sticky grenade. As the tank spun off its track a soldier with remarkable speed and pluck jumped on top of it and dropped a grenade down the turret.

But the Rangers were finished. With practically no ammunition, and very few men left alive or uninjured, they were attacked from all sides and even from the direction of their own lines. They had held out for many appalling hours until the end came. Only six men were able to escape out of the 767 men who had started the attack. Many were killed and the remainder taken prisoner. The Germans also suffered grievous losses. Nearly 300 men were killed, 465 wounded and 440 unaccounted for. Colonel Darby, who with General Truscott had been obliged to wait helplessy in a command bunker while messages came in, was overcome with grief. If only he could have died with his men! But it was one of the anomalies of war that a leader sometimes has to direct from base while sending his men into battle.

As the afternoon wore on it was clear that the enemy had halted the attack all along the seven mile front. The Americans had not expected such opposition, while the Germans had thrown their reserves piecemeal into every gap in their line. General Alexander meanwhile had ordered General Clarke to continue the attacks on the vital towns of Cisterna and Campoleone. These were to be the main strongholds of the beach-head and the anchors from which the two divisions were to break out towards Rome. It was equally important to enlarge the perimeter as the German artillery could still cover every inch of the terrain, including Anzio itself.

Before the General's order could be carried out, alarming intelligence reports were coming in indicating that a new massive counter-offensive was imminent by greatly reinforced German troops. Kesselring had assembled strong formations from the North of Italy, France and Yugo-Slavia, amounting to some 110,000 men. To urge him on, Hitler declared *'The Fuhrer expects the bitterest struggle for every yard.'* General Alexander appreciated that Kesselring could concentrate his armour and infantry at any point on the allied salient and might cut off all the forward forces, driving a wedge at the weakest point, and thrusting on to the coast. He therefore ordered General Lucas to call off all the planned attacks and concentrate on preparing a strong defensive ring all around the beach-head.

For a short while a strange quietness descended over the battlefield as the two armies awaited their coming ordeal. While the British and American divisions hastily erected barbed wire barriers and laid minefields under cover oif darkness, the Germans were preparing under Hitler's personal orders to drive the invaders back into the sea.

6
Backs to the Wall

The hours of that stormy night dragged on interminably. About three o'clock the noises of battle around us grew less and soon an uneasy silence made us apprehensive of any nearby sounds. When we heard footsteps approaching along the road, our sentries gave a loud challenge. Fortunately we soon recognised Major Bridgman and the Company Sergeant Major.

'A bit of good cheer for you all,' he greeted us. 'Bring out your mugs. We're to be given a rum ration.'

The CSM produced a flagon and began to pour a tot of rum into each man's tin mug. (Rum, common in the navy, was issued only in times of special need in the army.)

Within a few minutes the rum and packets of cigarettes were distributed to us all. 'What's been going on?' I asked Major Bridgman. 'Sounded like a hell of a battle just finished.'

'As far as I know the Germans have been attacking all around the bridgehead. We're in the middle here but soon we'll be in the thick of it.'

'Thanks for the good news. Will we get any breakfast?'

'Hard-tack biscuits if you're lucky. B Eschelon hasn't been able to get through with the rations – heavy shelling. Come on Sergeant Major, 11 Platoon next.'

They went on down the dark road. The rum together with their visit helped to restore our confidence in spite of the grim prospects.

At last came a watery dawn. By sunrise the clouds slowly cleared away and a fresh wind brought mingled smells of spent gunpowder and death. The Company Quarter-Master arrived in a Bren Carrier bringing hot tea, hard-tack and tins of bully beef. No fresh orders came through, so after changing the sentries we tried to get some much needed sleep lying on ground-sheets on the wet earth.

All day we remained there, cold and hungry, but at last able to sleep, oblivious of all that might be going on around us. The expected call to move on came as soon as it got dark. As no reserve troops were

Attack at dawn with tanks
beyond Horror Farm

Mopping up the enemy, past blazing German tank – February 1944

British war cemetery: Anzio on a rainy day

Ruins of monastery at Monte Cassino after bombing

The rebuilt Abbey overlooks the Allied War Cemetery at Monte Cassino

Tunisia, June 1944
Captain G. Reynolds Payne, The Author, Major L. Bridgman

Painted by a German prisoner of war, Ghardinaou, June 1943

The Author, 1943

Colonel of the Regiment with the Colonel-in-Chief
Lt-Gen Sir Peter Graham : HRH The Prince of Wales

Pipes and Drums in Rome
8th June 1944

6th Gordons in Tunisia

| Major | Capt | Col | Brig | The | Lt | Major |
| Bridgman | Hatt | Peddie | Moore | Author | Leckie | Williamson |

Roman Amphitheatre at foot of Monte Cassino escaped the bombing

Vesuvius: the eruption of May 1944
(See Epilogue pages 160 and 161)

available to meet the ever increasing enemy threat, we were to be sent to fill a gap in the line.

As B Company was the only remaining company of the Gordons we had a most responsible task ahead. The night was bright but cold, with a full moon turning the flooded fields into pools of silver. Tramping along an open road, we were met by an officer of the Reconnaissance Regiment.

'You won't need to stay long on this road,' he warned us. 'The Hun can see everything in the moonlight. He's been shelling the road all day.'

There was no cover to be had on either side, so we marched on quickly, until we reached a deserted hamlet called Padaglione, situated in the middle of a marshy plain. Here B Company was to establish a firm defensive position and to be ready for any enemy attack. Major Bridgman quickly allotted the platoon areas so that we could get our trenches dug before dawn. Ten Platoon was allocated a space around a few derelict farm buildings. In one of these we found a number of abandoned, squealing pigs who evidently hoped that we were their new owners. But now the moonlight gave us away. As soon as we started to dig in the squelchy soil, a shower of mortar bombs landed near the farm. Only two men were slightly injured but it became impossible to prepare any secure defences. The walls of buildings provided protection at least from view, so all we could do was to make firing slits through windows or holes in the walls.

Norman had meanwhile been ordered to take his platoon to fill another gap on the left of the Recce Regiment about a mile away from our farm. Some two hours before dawn I was called to see Major Bridgman.

'Norman seems to be in a tight corner,' he said. 'Message from the Recce Commander that he had a running fight with a German patrol and has only just reached his new position. The Bren Carrier which was to have brought up his ammunition and rations has been held up. It's just arrived here now. Will you take two men for unloading, and make a dash across in the carrier?'

'Now's a good time. The moon's going down.'

'Yes, but you've only got about half an hour before dawn. Get going at once.'

'Where's the stuff to be unloaded?'

'At the entrance to Norman's ditch. He'll have to carry it from there. You must get the carrier back before first light. Good luck!'

Telling Sergeant Maclaren to take over 10 Platoon, I with two other men who had volunteered, ran over to where the carrier was waiting. Unfortunately, as the moonlight faded the first streaks of dawn showed in the clear sky. I urged the driver to go fast before we became a clear target for the enemy gunners. As our carrier bumped and rattled across the open plain our hopes were dashed by the crash of the first shell bursting nearby. Mortars and machine guns were quick to range onto this inviting chance. Bullets, bomb splinters and mud splattered against the sides of the carrier, but somehow we reached the partial shelter of a ridge of high ground behind which the ditch ran.

While the men started to unload, I ran along the ditch to see Norman. The whole front had fully woken up now, and heavy firing came from all around. On reaching the left outpost of the Recce position, an officer shouted to me to go no further.

'There's a strong Jerry patrol approaching.' He warned me as we crouched in a water-logged ditch. 'They're trying to infiltrate between us and your platoon.' To emphasise his words a nearby burst of Bren fire clashed with the clatter of German Spandaus.

'I have to get through to them with their ammo and rations,' I insisted. 'Perhaps along this ditch – '

'If you tried now you'd only lose the lot. Wait until things quieten a little. As soon as we've beaten back the Jerries I'll detail a carrrying party to take the stuff up to them. Where is it now?'

'About a hundred yards back along the ditch. I've promised to get my carrier back safely.'

'Right, leave the stuff with us. We'll make sure it's quickly delivered.'

Another Spandau opened up, much nearer this time. I hurried back to where the carrier had already been unloaded and was waiting to return. So leaving the stores in the care of the Recce platoon the two men and I climbed back into the carrier for the dash back to our own company.

The light had quickly increased so we should make an excellent target for the waiting Germans. It was to be the most exciting ride of my whole life.

The driver revved up the engine and the carrier butted its nose above the sloping edge of the ditch. We had not gone more than a few yards before a succession of bangs sounded behind us. Then as the carrier was in full view on the wide plain, the enemy unleashed every weapon on this escaping quarry. Mortar bombs exploded all around us. We crouched down as low as possible as pieces of shrapnel and machine gun bullets crashed against the carrier's thin armour plating. It was impossible to remain entirely behind this cover, for the carrier was bumping and bucking over the uneven ground to such an extent that we were continually thrown upwards like stones in a sieve. The driver was magnificent, weaving a zig-zag course to evade the missiles. It seemed as though he knew exactly where the next mortar bombs were going to land. As he turned, the carrier lurched drunkenly, and its tracks chewed the earth, the engine whining in protest.

At last we reached the haven of low ground in a valley where B Company HQ was situated. Major Bridgman was standing anxiously waiting. 'Thank God you're all safe!' he exclaimed, 'Sounded as though they were throwing everything they had at you.'

'Yes but Norman's in a bad way.' I quickly described what had happened, 'Will you let me take my platoon and see if I can help him?'

'By the time you get there it may be too late – so let's hope that with the help of the Recce they've driven off the German patrol. Wait a moment – I'll try and get the CO on the air.' He went over to the signaller and within a few moments was speaking to Battalion HQ. Then with a grim expression he turned to me.

'We are to do nothing yet. The CO is in touch with the Recce Commander. It seems that the Germans have put down a smoke screen and the Recce are expecting an attack at any moment. You'd better return to your platoon and stand by till I call you.'

I returned to my platoon where Sergeant Maclaren had organised an all round defence area with weapons sited to fire through windows and round the corners of walls. Here we waited for nearly an hour while a sharp outburst of firing came from the direction of the Recce Regiment and Norman's platoon. Then as the sounds of battle went ominously silent, I saw a column of smoke arising as though a smoke screen had been laid. Soon a message came for me to return to Company HQ where Major Bridgman was speaking on the wireless. Then putting down the earphones he looked haggard and weary as he turned to me. 'The message has come through at last,' he said. 'Norman and all his platoon have been lost. The enemy put in a strong attack under cover of smoke. Cut Norman completely off. The Recce Company tried to cut their way through but when the smoke cleared away there was no one left. That's all I know. We must hope they're safe as prisoners.' (After the war Norman and all his platoon were safely repatriated from German prison camps, except for two men who had been killed in a running fight with the German patrol, which had infiltrated behind the ditch and then cut off Norman's platoon while under cover of the smoke screen.)

Now, of the whole battalion only my own platoon and No 11 remained. Major Bridgman warned me to expect further enemy attacks at any moment, so I hurried back to the cluster of farm buildings. Ten Platoon was on the left of B Company positions, with eleven Platoon, commanded by a sergeant, being dug in on a slight rise to our right. My two forward sections had a good field of fire from a stable, while the third was in a pigsty. This latter made a useful if odorous defensive position, the walls being of solid bricks with slits through which we could point our weapons. The original inhabitants of the sty were unceremoniously herded into a nearby shed, where they remained grunting and squealing throughout the day. Behind this sty, I established an OP which commanded a clear view across the plain.

No sooner had we settled into our new quarters, than the first salvo of mortar bombs started falling. This was a clear warning that the Germans had moved into the offensive. With a mere handful of troops spread out in this sector, the defence was not going to be easy.

During that long day, the Germans seemed content to pulverise our location with artillery and mortar fire. The continual whine of shells and the shattering blast of explosions all around us made life very nerve racking. Somehow the walls of the farm buildings withstood the blast. One direct hit killed two men in 11 Platoon, but almost miraculously no one else was hurt. Major Bridgman only just escaped when flying shrapnel smashed his wireless set. With this last link of communication gone we were truly isolated, without news and without orders.

At the end of the day tensely waiting for an attack which never came, we were greatly relieved when under cover of darkness a dinner of hot stew was brought to us. 'At least we shan't have to kill one of our prize pigs to cook roast pork,' commented Hayward our cook. The pigs seemed to have heard him for they set up a renewed chorus of loud squealing.

After this meal, which we ate ravenously, we were able to dig new slit trenches outside the farm as the rising moon was hidden by clouds. This gave us better protection against shelling next day.

It seemed that we had finished digging just in time, for the night was suddenly lit by bright flashes from enemy artillery. All the guns had opened up between us and the hills of Rome. The whine of shells passed away to our left, indicating that an attack was being launched between us and the sea, no doubt with the object of driving a wedge between our forces. After the guns had been pounding for an hour, we heard the sudden stutter of machine guns. Yellow tracer bullets crossed each other in a mad medley of fury.

All this time we stood in our trenches and behind the walls of the farm expecting the offensive to come our way. But instead, we were deluged by a sudden thunderstorm. Forked lightning fllashed from black clouds and the thunder roared with greater fury than the guns. Soon the rain began to fall in torrents, filling our newly dug trenches, adding to our misery. The storm and the battle continued for some hours. As far as we could tell, the enemy were making no great progress, for the heaviest fighting seemed still in the same area near the coast. Our own immediate front was inactive, except for a machine gun which kept firing just over our heads.

Towards dawn the sounds of fighting grew less, but the rain had ruined our positions. The flat ground was turned into a lake and all our trenches hidden beneath the water. Once again we were issued with a rum ration which warmed our throats for a short while. As the light grew we resumed our old places in the farm buildings and ate our cold breakfast.

That day dragged on interminably. The enemy, seeing that our farm presented the only obstacle to them in the surrounding plain, began to shell it systematically. Our stout walls could no longer resist the blast of the heavier shells. Our pigsty remained intact, but the stable was soon breached with large holes. A stall used as a temporary Aid Post contained a growing number of wounded lying on dirty straw.

The stable having been reduced mainly to rubble, I moved two of my sections into the downstairs rooms of the deserted Italian farmhouse. This was in a state of total confusion, having been abandoned in haste as the battle drew near. Household goods were scattered over the floor, but an open cupboard revealed a small hoard of American K rations, acquired no doubt from generous doughboys before the real fighting began. The most enticing pieces of furniture were three large beds complete with sheets and blanket. If only we could have thrown ourselves down on that softness and slept!

Just as I was looking longingly at these beds a shout came from a sentry. 'Tanks, sir!' he exclaimed. 'Coming out of the woods.' Looking through the window I saw two German Tiger tanks lumbering out of the wooded country towards us. If these Leviathans decided to attack our flimsy fortress, we should be blasted to pieces within a few minutes.

Without the wireless, the only way I could inform Major Bridgman was by sending Wilson to warn him of this latest danger. As always when the situation was at its most critical, Lindsay Bridgman remained in his coolest and most light-hearted mood. No one could lose hope while he remained at the head of the company. In a few minutes Wilson returned with a scribbled note which I read to my platoon to everyone's encouragement:

'When you've knocked out the tanks don't bag all the loot. Reserve a Luger for me. Did you have a good dinner?'

I remained in the shadow of the farmhouse window anxiously watching the progress of the tanks. For a short while they paused behind a clump of trees as though awaiting further orders. Then a line of infantry appeared moving up towards the tanks. Both then began a steady movement forward. I sent another message to Major Bridgman:

'Tigers approaching us slowly. Infantry emerging from woods. Have a good seat in the pavilion here. Will let you know lunch scores. Yes, lovely grub. Found stack of US rations.'

'Is your PIAT well sited and camouflaged?' came the reply. 'Don't fire till last moment. Beast! Hope you are sick!'

The leading tank opened fire on us at a range of half a mile. The shell from its 88mm gun knocked the front wall out of an unoccupied farm cottage next to our farmhouse. Two other nearby cottages suffered a similar fate. Our turn would come next. I quickly withdrew all the men from the exposed walls and, taking what shelter might remain in the rear of the building, waited until the tank turned its attention elsewhere. The tank commander evidently considered that one shot would be enough. With a great crash the front room of the farmhouse was blown to bits, leaving overhanging rafters poised ready to collapse at any moment. There still remained enough cover to resume firing positions against any infantry attack. So behind partly shattered walls and mounds of rubble we awaited whatever might be coming.

From my window I was able to observe the tanks advancing. They came within a quarter of a mile and then veered off to their right, passing our farm buildings as though satisfied that they had destroyed as much of them as was necessary. As our platoon wireless set as well as the company set had been destroyed by the shelling, there was no way we could warn the troops behind of the tanks' approach, nor of trying to stop them. We could only watch the tanks move past our farm and out of sight behind us.

It was then the turn of the enemy infantry. Assuming perhaps that the tanks had destroyed everyone in the farm buildings they advanced boldly across the open plain in open formation, their bayonets fixed, and looking extremely formidable! As far as I could tell there must have been at least 200 men.

Our only chance to keep them off was to bluff them. To make them think we were a much stronger force than we were had worked before, so I hastily gave the men their orders. 'Keep hidden; keep quiet. Wait for my signal, then give the buggers everything you've got!'

Every man waited tensely with his weapon aimed through windows or behind the rubble. The enemy approached nearer, heading directly towards our farm. On a rough estimate we were outnumbered by about eight to one. But the enemy looked over-confident, and were presenting a good target. I let them reach a point about a hundred yards distant, and yelled 'FIRE!'

Every Bren, rifle and two inch mortar, let off a simultaneous blast. On our right an equal burst of fire came from No 11 platoon. This sudden salvo seemed to knock the enemy over like startled rabbits. Every man went to ground, although we could not tell whether many had been hit. Some fired their rifles in our direction as they crawled backwards, others could be seen helping the wounded and dragging them to safer positions.

Our firing ceased after the initial burst so that they would be kept guessing as to our strength. We remained, we hoped, an unknown threat waiting to strike again if they came near. These tactics seemed to succeed at least for a short while, but we knew that the Germans would quickly reorganise and probably launch a new more concentrated attack.

Then to our intense relief, shells from our own artillery landed near them. These were no doubt ranging rounds after some bright artillery officer had realised what was happening, for within moments another cluster of shells landed in their midst. A German

Red Cross ambulance ventured forward and we watched several wounded being hurried away to safety. The remainder of the infantry began to dig in about three hundred yards from us.

The attack had thus been halted by our two platoons pretending to be much stronger than we were, but the bluff could not last very long. The next shock came from the German artillery. Suddenly our battered farmhouse received a shattering blow. A tremendous explosion shook the building, bringing down bricks, rubble and choking dust on top of us. Shouts for stretcher bearers rang out and groans from the wounded. It was a terrible moment, but we could do nothing but hang on in the vain hope that no more shells would add to the carnage. I went to see the injured men as they were being given first aid by Gordon and Hadden, the two stretcher bearers. 'They need to be got away, sir,' said Gordon. 'There's not much we can do.'

One man had died; his body was still lying there with a ground sheet thrown over it. Three other men needed urgent treatment; one with a head injury, one with a broken hip, and a third whose leg had been blown off below the knee. In spite of morphia they were suffering greatly.

Until Major Bridgman returned from visiting No 11 Platoon, I sat down on the straw by them trying to assure them that help was on its way. The man with the leg blown off was more worried by the prospect of returning home a cripple than by the pain.

Soon Major Bridgman returned. 'We'll have to get an ambulance,' he said after looking round the wounded men, 'but the road is under continual shellfire. I doubt if anything could get along it during daylight, even if we could get a message through.'

I went through to the adjoining stable to see if there was any hope of repairing the damaged wireless set.

'It's no use, sir, we need a new set,' reported the signaller.

At that moment a Jock from No 11 Platoon looked into the stable. He was a small man, not much over five feet in height. He had left his pack off but was carrying his rifle. As we looked up from the damaged wireless set, he said to Major Bridgman in a determined but matter-of-fact tone, 'Excuse me sir, but I'm just going to fetch an ambulance.'

At any other time it might have seemed strange for a private soldier quietly to tell his company commander that he was going off on his own. But now no one could have wished for a finer example of calm resolution in order to help his friends.

'All right, Sinclair,' agreed Major Bridgman, 'but how are you going to get across the open plain?'

'I'll get through, sir,' replied Sinclair calmly.

'Very well. Good luck.'

We watched him run a short distance and jump into a shallow ditch. Then crouching down he progressed alongside the road until he was lost to view as the road turned a corner.

I returned to my platoon to be ready for any new advance from the enemy. No further tanks appeared, and the infantry had dug themselves in about 300 yards away.

Sinclair had meanwhile evidently managed to crawl or dash across the plain to reach Battalion HQ, for within an hour of his departure an ambulance appeared on the deserted road. Although its Red Cross was plainly visible it was taking a great risk in driving along this shell-pitted coverless plain. However, it was allowed to pass unmolested and reached our farm without a shot being fired.

What a relief it was to get those wounded men to where they could be properly looked after! For many hours they had lain in that filthy stable, while the shells had been exploding all around. Now dusk was beginning to bring more dark clouds, and the rain fell once again. We faced another night of isolation, and the prospect of the inevitable attack on our farm at dawn or before. No rations could be brought to us along the exposed road, so we were more than pleased that we had found the American K rations – enough for each man to have half a meal.

About nine o'clock a runner got through to us from Colonel Peddie. The message he brought was short, but completely revived our flagging spirits: 'British line being formed behind you by midnight. Withdraw at 0100 hours.'

The remaining four hours passed like a distorted dream. The lack of sleep for so long had dulled our minds and made the suspense less acute. Anyone of us could have fallen into sleep even when standing up. As the wind arose, the driving rain penetrated the holes in the shattered buildings, but at least these miserable conditions seemed to have discouraged the enemy from renewing their attacks.

I went round to visit the men in the pigsty and then returned to the rest of the platoon in the dark stable. Soon I must have fallen asleep. In a dazed condition I suddenly became aware that something cold and wet was being pressed against my face. As in a dream I imagined this to be the muzzle of a Tiger Tank's gun aimed to fire at me.

Waking in alarm I found myself lying in the straw beneath the sleepy damp nose of a cow! The bewildered animal backed away as I sat up, no doubt puzzled by the strange intruders to her home.

Midnight came, and at last at one o'clock we assembled in silence outside the pigsty and the stable. With no regrets but still in a vaguely dazed condition we left the farm which had been a partial haven during those ghastly hours, and marched in single file along the road. It was now so dark that we could hardly even make out the shape of the man in front.

All night we tramped on, following a circuitous route, avoiding cross-roads and other possible fixed targets for enemy shells. When morning came we were directed into a wood about a mile behind another sector of the front line. Even here we could get little rest or sleep, for our own artillery was hidden in these woods. The noise of these guns continually firing would not have kept us awake, but the enemy retaliated and so we had to dig new trenches as fast as possible for protection in the midst of the artillery duels.

Then we were bombed. The Luftwaffe, becoming increasingly active, roared over the woods, trying to put our guns out of action. It was dangerous to move about in the woods, as many unexploded butterfly bombs were hidden like booby-traps in the trees and bushes.

For one night we were left in this so-called 'rest' area, sleeping soundly at the bottom of our trenches, too exhausted to be disturbed by the artillery fire which continued all night. At dawn the German planes returned and hurriedly dropped their bombs in and around our woods before being ignominiously chased away by a squadron of Spitfires. As far as we were concerned, they only served to rouse us in time for a welcome breakfast of porridge and sausage. So for one morning at least we were well fed and our wet battle dress had almost dried out, for which small mercies we were more than grateful.

While we were thus temporarily uncommitted, a great deal of activity was taking place in both the German and British Command Headquarters. Field Marshal Kesselring was under intense pressure from Hitler to score a great and immediate victory by 'lancing the abcess' and eradicating the poison of the allied invasion. Kesselring, in his turn, had to spur on von Mackensen to prepare the Fourteenth Army for an all-out offensive. As a result, a final plan, named 'Fishchfang' ('fish-catching') was drawn up. The original idea for coastal attacks to cut off our forces from their sea-borne supplies was discarded, as the Germans realised that their forces would be heavily shelled from the allied warships. They therefore decided on a concentrated attack by two corps down the route of the Via Anziate, using the Factory and the town of Carroceto as harbours for tanks. At the same time, the 1st Parachute Corps would attack on the west flank to put the Allies under intense pressure. As a centre spearhead of the offensive Hitler decided to send from Germany his special regiment made up of selected Nazis, the Infantry Lehr Regiment. It was decided that this great battle should begin on 16th February.

General Lucas, meanwhile, had a clear perception of the options open to the Germans, especially when on 11th February the Thunderbirds of the US 45th Division atttempted to recapture the Factory and found it heavily defended. The 179th Regiment suffered grievous casualties. As the enemy therefore still held the Factory in great strength, Lucas fixed a reserve defence line on either side of the Fly-over, some three miles south of Carroceto station. If the Germans broke through this line they had only the Padiglione Woods (our 'rest' area) between there and Anzio town. The main defenders of this line were the 45th US Division under General Eagles and the 56th British Division under General Templer. Behind them, in reserve for the moment, was the much battered 1st British Division. Although the two armies were thus poised for the critical battles to come there was no lessening of the fighting all around the beachhead.

Our period of rest lasted exactly one morning. We were required to fill a gap in the line somewhere in the direction of Rome, so on a gloomy afternoon we set out once again along muddy tracks until after several hours we reached our new positions feeling wet and bedraggled. My platoon's area was to be on top of a slight hill overlooking a valley. Beneath us was an intricate system of caves dug deep in the hillside opening into the valley. As our Company HQ was situated in the centre of these dark catacombs, I first had to find my way into their sombre interior, in order to see Major Bridgman.

'Welcome to our new home, Ted,' he said. 'We can get some idea of what the early Christians must have felt in their caves.'

'They only had lions to face when they went out. We may have a worse reception.'

'You may be right. Anyway, let me show you the interior.' With the aid of a torch, he led the way down into the centre of the hill. Apart from the torch's beam the blackness was intense. We reached what appeared to be a subterranean dungeon. The darkness had now changed to a lurid red light which leaped and flickered from several bonfires burning empty shell-cases. The rough, rocky walls of the cave glowed as though we had been spirited into the infernal regions.

These phantasmagorial effects were heightened by the figures moving through the shadow; soldiers with dirty bearded faces were preparing to leave after we had taken over from them. Some were fully dressed and equipped, others were packing their haversacks in the light of the flames, or throwing more shell-cases to feed the fire. In one corner wounded men were lying, where the stretcher bearers had recently laid them awaiting the arrival of the doctor.

'We may be here a few days,' Major Bridgman informed me. 'Reinforcements are on their way to make our company up to strength. Meanwhile we are acting as a kind of long-stop to prevent the enemy infiltrating round the flanks. By all accounts it won't be easy with only two platoons. German patrols are active every night.'

After receiving my orders, I went out once again to get my platoon in position on the top of the hill. We watched the unit whose places we were taking, departing silently, leaving us alone in the darkness and the rain.

For three days and nights we remained. The days were long and dreary as we sheltered from occasional shell fire and heard the sounds of battle coming from the area we had left. During the hours of darkness we waited fully alert in our muddy trenches while the enemy continually pounded us with shells and mortar bombs. Every night a strong attack or fighting patrol was sent against different parts of the line. But each time our machine guns, artillery and mortars, firing their SOS tasks, broke up the attacks before they could penetrate our defences. During these attacks we in our trenches added rifle and Bren gun fire whenever the Germans looming up in the darkness presented a fair target. Overhead, the dark sky was frequently lit with the glare of flares dropped by planes, both British and German, that flew over the battlefield to bomb both the front and rear areas. Behind us the anti-aircraft defences of Anzio harbour sent up a dazzling display of fireworks, while in the distance the chains of yellow tracer seemed to glide lazily up into the dark void.

It was only during certain hours of the day that we were able to leave the exposed hilltop in order to take a hot meal and try to rest in the caves. What a strange unreal existence! As usual, no one was able to get any real sleep. Only an occasional hour snatched from the eternal vigilance enabled us to keep alert during this endless time.

On the third day a new platoon of reinforcements came to take the place of Norman's missing place in the company. No sooner had they dug new trenches for themselves, than a new and exceptionally violent attack began with a deluge of mortar bombs. A strong German fighting patrol swept round from the right flank – just as we had been warned to expect. It was a severe baptism of fire for the newcomers, and sadly several were either killed or wounded in their first hour of facing the enemy. Two men of my platoon received head injuries from shrapnel, but in spite of casualties we drove off the attack. The Germans withdrew leaving several men dead and others injured whom they managed to carry away with them.

As the night gave way to a grey, cheerless dawn, we were encouraged to see how well the new platoon had stood up to their first battle. Shaken but determined, they knew that Anzio would test them to the uttermost, but as yet they had not learnt to take life (and death) as it came, with the stoic but indifferent fatalism of the old soldier.

During my rounds visiting my section positions, I felt particularly proud of those few remaining men who had been with the platoon from the start, some of whom had been wounded, absent a while and returned; Craig and Watson, Reay, my batman, Chisholm, Cope, Forbes, MacDonald, Hayward, Corporals Tripney, Allardyce and Boyes, and the dependable Sergeant Maclaren. Everyone was able to grumble and swear with a sense of humour, and restore the newcomers' confidence with a reassuring contempt for the enemy's chances of breaking through. When the enemy machine guns shattered the darkness, uncomfortably close, Tripney, Boyes and Allardyce would keep their men alert but unscared; Sergeant Maclaren's stolid unconcern always seemed to lessen the dangers; while the cheerful and defiant outbursts of swearing from the men all helped to maintain the confidence of the whole platoon.

At last these few interminable days on this hill came to an end. At midnight on the 13th February an American battalion arrived to relieve us. Unlike us, with a dour and fatalistic sense of humour, the Yanks were full of bombastic confidence and aggression. 'We're gonna pump lead into those sons of bitches. We'll kill every goddam Kraut and damn Hitler to hell.' One felt almost sorry for the poor Germans up against such fearsome warriors.

The take-over was effected not without difficulty, for the enemy planes were dropping flares to guide their bombers, and the usual spasmodic shelling made all movements risky. However, by 2am we marched once more back into the Padiglione woods to prepare for the onslaught to come. The two days behind the line gave us no rest as the Germans' artillery kept up a continual bombardment against our own guns and supply lines.

On the second morning a shell landed directly into the slit trench occupied by Jimmy Leckie, the Signals Officer, who was killed instantly, and Jimmy Methven, Intelligence, who was seriously injured. (He survived the war but never fully recovered from the wounds.) This was a very sad blow for us all, and for me in particular, as they were both my good friends. It emphasised yet again how impossible it was to find anywhere on the beach-head safe from bombs and shells. We were almost glad when the order came for us to advance once more and take up new defensive positions in readiness for the long expected German offensive.

7
The German Offensive

From midnight on the 16th February, the guns went silent. An eerie hush took the place of the usual thunder of artillery; even the wind dropped and the sky cleared, allowing a frost to develop before dawn. All the men waiting shivering in their foxholes knew that with first light must come the beginning of a new and perhaps final bombardment. The dark hours passed in grim suspense, with nothing to do but stare into the distance, imagining that every tree or bush was moving nearer.

As six o'clock exactly came the long expected roar of guns. The entire orchestra of German artillery opened up in a crashing paroxysm of fury. In an ear-splitting drum roll of explosions the shells landed in and all around the Allied lines.

For half an hour this broadside lasted. Then followed an equally sudden silence. After the guns came the German infantry supported by tanks. In closely packed waves they surged forwards, the main thrust, as expected, being down and alongside the Anzio-Albano road.

The British and American artillery were more than ready. With a far more concentrated fire power than the Germans, they unleashed a terrible vengeance on the enemy infantry who fell in hundreds. But there were always more to follow, more men rushing into the slaughter in waves driving against the waiting defenders.

All morning the attack lasted. Hitler's special troops, the Infantry Lehr, were almost decimated by the fearful rain of shells and the incessant machine gun fire. All their officers were killed and the men, now leaderless, were forced back behind their start-line. But the 179th US Regimental Combat Team had also suffered severe casualties in the attack. They had held out bravely in the face of six German divisions, but the sheer weight of infantry, Tiger tanks and the German guns had almost succeeded in driving through their lines.

At the end of the day, both sides had suffered terrible losses, yet neither could claim a decisive victory. During the night the Germans launched yet another fierce attack, this time the darkness provided sufficient cover for the infantry to infiltrate between the US battalions. By first light a German brigade rammed home this advantage in a concentrated attack along the axis of the Anzio-Albano road. All morning a fierce battle raged. In spite of severe casualties the Germans forced their way through the Allied defences and fanned out to their left and right, thus establishing a critical bulge like a hernia in the Allied line. To implement their land forces the Luftwaffe managed to evade the Spitfires and sent waves of Focke-Wulfs and Messerschmitt fighter bombers to strafe the defenders.

GERMAN OFFENSIVE, 18 FEBRUARY 1944

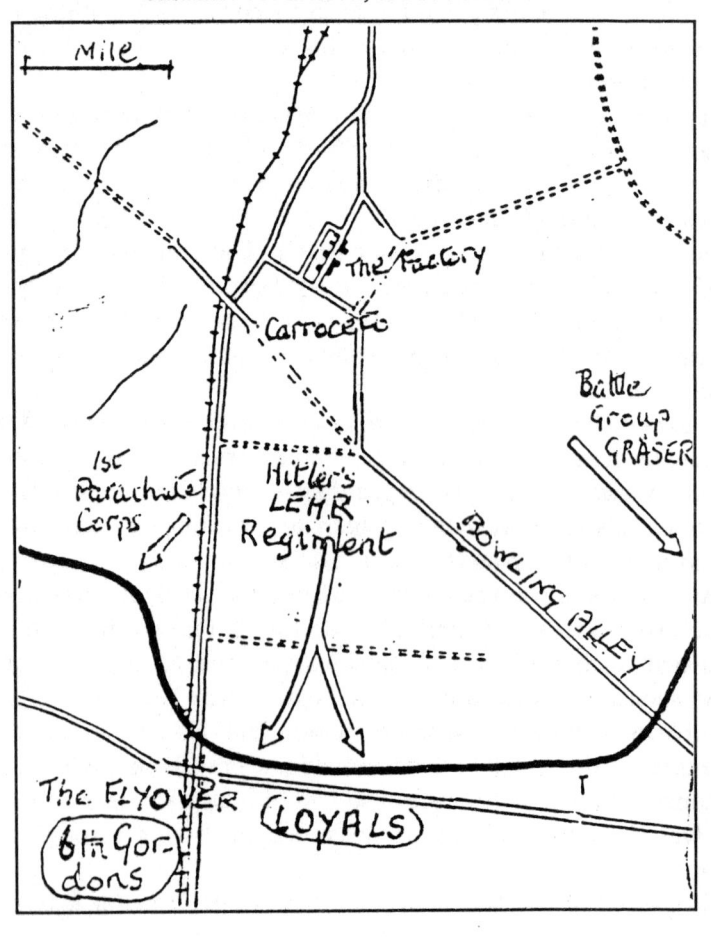

General Clarke realised that the beach-head was in grave danger. From their newly won positions the Germans had only to drive further south, overwhelm the final defence line around the Flyover and thrust their way to Anzio harbour. Clarke had one card left up his sleeve; he had managed to persuade General Saville of the 12th Air Support Command to divert heavy bombers from tasks over Southern Germany to fly down to Anzio. So on this critical day, 17 February, squadrons of Flying Fortresses, Wellingtons and Liberators dropped a huge weight of bombs on the German infantry and tanks all around the Campoleone, Albano area. The havoc caused was devastating. Many casualties and much damage resulted from this new and unexpected inferno. Yet still the Germans came on, as more troops were thrown into the cauldron. The Allied line was forced backwards to the last line of resistance around the Flyover. General Lucas had no option but to move every man and every unit to defend the beach-head from total collapse; this included what remained of the 1st Division to fill a gap on the right flank of the US Regimental Team around the Flyover.

Back in the Padiglione Woods we listened amazed to the sounds of the stupendous battle being waged only a few miles to the north. Then we looked up into the clear sky and saw wave after wave of the heavy Flying Fortress and Wellington bombers dropping a huge concentration of bombs. The earth shook and billows of smoke rose from a wide area.

It came as no surprise when a message arrived from General Penney to all units in the Division: 'Stand by in immediate readiness to move forward to resist enemy action.'

Almost as soon as this message was received, the order came to fall in and march up the main Anzio-Rome road as far as the Flyover. Here B Company was to establish two platoons on the left of the road, while 11 Platoon, under Sergeant Mitchell, was sent out on a standing patrol to remain all night in front of the Flyover.

As soon as we reached our new area we began to dig as fast as possible, as shells were falling haphazardly all over the open ground. I was soon called to see Major Bridgman whose HQ was now behind a clump of trees, unprotected from shellfire.

'I've just been for Orders from Colonel Peddie,' he told me. 'The Germans are forcing their way through a wide gap just in front of us. We're part of the last ditch defence. No retreat. On the right of the

Flyover the Loyals are digging in. Tonight the American General Harmon is to make a counter-attack with tanks to relieve the pressure. Let's hope he succeeds. That's all I know at the moment. So keep alert all night.'

I hurried back to my platoon to make sure that every man was ready in well-sited defence positions. As soon as dark gave some protection, a Bren carrier risked the spasmodic shells and brought us the first meal of the day, a hot stew which we ate ravenously. Then came the long night. For hour after hour we waited, gazing into the darkness, watching the incessant flashes from artillery followed by explosions in front of us and the criss-crossing of tracer bullets as the Germans intensified their attack.

Then on our right a new clash of fire power came from much nearer. The Loyals were evidently fighting off a direct attack on the far side of the Flyover. Machine guns, Brens, Spandaus, rifles, guns and grenades all mingled in a deafening pandemonium. In our trenches we waited grimly expecting the battle to reach us at any moment. Sure enough, at about three in the morning dark shadows loomed against the skyline as a strong German patrol advanced towards us. We were ready with our well-tried tactics of waiting until the last moment and then blasting off with a broadside from all our weapons. The dark shapes fell to the ground. German shouts and cries for help indicated that the patrol had been halted. In the confusion we saw through the darkness that men were being carried away and the remainder of the Germans disappeared the way they had come.

So the nightmare ended – for the moment. A nightmare it was, for the dark shapes coming nearer in the darkness, with rifles, grenades and bayonets, were to bring injury and death in their path. Instead, they met death themselves, such was the perversity of war, for they were men like us, with parents, wives and families of their own. Kill or be killed; repulse the enemy or allow him to break through the line and surge on to conquer; that was the only rule of war, as it always had been throughout the centuries.

During the few remaining hours before dawn, the guns gradually went silent. A sombre hush descended over the battlefield, with no sounds except the steady rainfall on sodden earth.

With the first glimmer of light, Mennim suddenly appeared beside me to fetch me to Company HQ. Major Bridgman was waiting in his calm, cold, yet half humorous battle mood.

'Things have not gone well during the night,' he said. 'The counter-attack never got started, mainly because the tanks got stuck in the quagmire and the infantry were driven back. As you will have heard, the Loyals have had a pasting all night. We've lost all contact with them, so the CO wants you to take a few men to the other side of the Flyover and find out what's happened.'

As he spoke, a salvo of shells erupted along the road and around the bridge. 'So the enemy have woken up again,' he added. 'More shelling. You'd better take an umbrella. Good luck.'

Within a few minutes I set out with Corporal Tripney and three men to try to reach the Loyals' position. Owing to our own minefields, the only way to reach them was to cross the road by the Flyover and hope to dodge the shells. Reaching the road, we took shelter in a ditch in order to look around. Two American tanks and a jeep were knocked out and smouldering. One of these tanks afforded a certain amount of protection from which I could get a better view of the surroundings. Through my binoculars I saw a few British troops near a much battered cottage. No Germans could be seen, but some hidden machine guns were firing across the open plains and right down our road making the Flyover even more unhealthy.

Returning to the ditch I ordered Corporal Tripney to give covering fire if necessary, while Wilson and I made a dash to join the few British troops. Fortune favoured us at that moment for the shelling ceased just as we had to cross the Flyover. The machine gunner, too, decided he had fired enough for the time being, so Wilson and I made a dash for it and reached the cottage without trouble.

The grimy, unshaven face of a corporal looked round a partly demolished wall as we approached. He challenged us with his rifle, clearly in a state of shock, a trickle of blood running down his forehead. 'Where the hell did you come from?' he demanded.

'The Gordons, on your left. Where's your Company commander?'

'In Heaven. I'm commanding this platoon. We've got seven men left.'

'How's the situation?'

'We're OK for the moment. They infiltrated between our platoons during the night, but we drove them off as soon as it got light.'

'Do you need any help now?'

'Yes, about ten men are lying wounded inside this old house. The rest are dead, including the officers. We also have one wounded German. He says our artillery killed more than half his company as soon as they started their attack.'

'Right, I'll let our CO know what happened. We'll try to send ambulances up for the wounded.'

'Thanks chum. Three of them are in a pretty bad way.'

'We'll do our best, Good luck.'

Wilson and I left the corporal who went back inside the cottage, no doubt to let the wounded know that help was on the way. We ran back across the road and past the Flyover. Joining Corporal Tripney we all hurried to get clear of the danger area. No sooner had we left the road than the machine guns opened up again with furious bursts. A moment later a salvo of shells crashed down on the ditch where we had sheltered. We quickly reached our lines, pleased with our good fortune and the temporary forbearance of the enemy gunners.

Within a few more minutes I was with Major Bridgman and on the field telephone to Colonel Peddie. 'The Loyals have had a severe battering,' I reported. 'In one company all the officers were killed and many of the men. Ten men are lying wounded in the cottage and urgently request ambulances. But in spite of all that they have held firm and driven back the enemy.'

'I'll do all I can,' Colonel Peddie reassured me, 'but ambulances are in much demand at the moment. Meanwhile you'd better get back to your platoon. The enemy is expected to launch his major attack alongside the road and past the Flyover.'

Back in my own lines, I found the men unexpectedly cheerful in spite of all the threats from the enemy. Breakfast that morning was particularly welcome – tinned sausage, hard-tack with butter and hot tea. I looked round at the men, tired, bedraggled, mud spattered, but utterly staunch and resilient. The old sweats were swearing but laughing as well, while the recent reinforcements showed a somewhat dazed but respectful pleasantness. What more could an officer wish for his men other than the hope that one day they would return home?

Even war sometimes throws up its tricks. As I was drinking my last mug of tea, a stray shell landed nearby scattering showers of mud in all directions. Something hit me with a dull thud on my bottom. Looking down I found a large, jagged piece of shrapnel, which had been so spent it had not even penetrated my greatcoat. This added to the general merriment, and seemed a symbol of the futility of the German's efforts.

This brief interlude of course did not last long. Shells soon began to fall more fequently. Between the explosions came the ominous rumble of tanks gradually growing louder. I went round my platoon. Everyone was waiting in his trench, fully aware that this was the last defence line between the enemy and the sea.

For General von Mackensen, 18 February was the most critical day of the German offensive. So far his massed forces had achieved a significant breakthrough south of Carroceto and the Factory, but at a crippling cost in manpower. Several German divisions, including the formidable Panzer, and Panzer Grenadier divisions with an infantry and the Jäger Division, had achieved their initial objectives, but had been prevented from making the final breakthrough which Hitler had ordered. So now von Mackensen drew on his reserves, made up the losses and ordered a great and final offensive to annihilate the Allied beach-head. The bad weather favoured the Germans, for persistent low cloud and rain prevented the Allied air forces from straffing or bombing the attackers. It was therefore left to the Allied artillery, with the infantry waiting tensely behind, to be the main defenders of the beach-head.

The offensive began with a three-pronged attack; the Battle Group Gräser storming south-east along the disused railway named Bowling Alley against the US 180 Regimental Combat Team. Their right wing began with the 1st Parachute Corps driving across the Lateral Road towards the Padiglione Woods, defended by the 157th RCT. The main thrust in the centre from Carroceto down the Via Anziate to the Flyover was headed by Hitler's favourite Lehr Regiment, which had been reinforced after their initial battering. Against this awe-inspiring attacking force, the Allied troops around the Flyover were the already depleted Loyals and what remained of the 6th Gordons. Had von Mackensen known the strength of the opposition, he must have been feeling very optimistic.

There was, however, one great hazard which the Germans had to overcome: for some two miles south of their start line, the country was flat and exposed with no natural cover. To protect his troops across this danger area, von Mackensen ordered his artillery to deliver a deluge of shells to blast the defenders' positions. The battle thus began with a fearsome German bombardment just as their infantry and tanks moved south from a line behind Carroceto.

Sheltering in our trenches we knew that this was the death-struggle on which the fate of the beach-head depended. However much we had experienced shellfire the terror never diminished. The shriek of the shells flashing ovehead, the fury of the explosions nearby and the terrible cry of wounded men, were nerve-searing beyond imagination.

Then came a new sound; instead of the shells racing at us from the enemy, a colossal outburst came from behind, from our own artillery. General Clarke had anticipated the German plan and had lined up every gun on the beach-head to concentrate fire on the exposed plain. The result was a torrent of shellfire on top of the advancing Germans, which must have been terrifying even to the bravest troops. From our trenches we saw the thousands of blinding flashes, while the thunderous roar sounded as though the entire earth were erupting.

Yet on the attacking troops came. Many must have perished beneath the rain of death, yet more were thrust into the furnace. Battalion after battalion rushed across the open plain either to be mown down by the intense fire, or to reach our own lines to face well sited machine guns and rifle fire.

All day the battle continued. More and more enemy troops managed through sheer weight of numbers to climb over their own dead and attack our defences. All along the line the fanatical infantry hurled themselves against us, in some places overrunning our thinly held positions, but unable to establish a secure foot-hold. Towards evening the attacks grew less intense. The battlefield was layered with German soldiers lying dead or waiting to be rescued by stretcher bearers. In our own trenches we had suffered severely from the onslaught. The Germans had thrown grenades, and peppered us with rifle and Spandau bullets and charged with bayonets until they themselves had fallen. But still they had not achieved the total victory they needed.

The night brought the blessing of darkness to enable both sides to gather in their wounded and collect the dead. It was a tragic day, reminiscent of some of the worst days of the First World War, and as it ended we knew that the end was not yet in sight. Tomorrow might be just as bad.

In my own platoon we had sustained fewer casualties than the Loyals on our right, who once again had faced the full fury of the attack. We had been fortunate in being on a slight rise and therefore able to fire down on the attackers. Corporal Allardyce had been wounded as well as four men, but none seriously. We all of course were drained of strength and shattered by the ferocity of the battle.

By midnight, in spite of all the difficulties, a Bren carrier got through to us with a cauldron of hot stew which helped not only to satisfy our hunger but to calm our distraught minds. Soon after, Major Bridgman and Colonel Peddie came to visit the Company and to ensure that all the wounded had been evacuated. In the darkness we could not see their faces, but their voices were normal and reassuring. 'You've all done very well so far,' said James Peddie. 'How are the men?'

'In good shape, sir. Don't like the shells, but we can cope.'

'Good show, but there may be more tomorrow. The good news is that a counter-attack by the Americans is going to start at first light – may relieve the pressure on us.'

'Thank God for the Yanks,' I replied. 'But what happened to the Loyals, sir? Sounded as though they had a terrible battering.'

'The only reports so far say they have held the line. Hand to hand fighting. Many casualties on both sides.'

'And the rest of our Brigade?'

'Much the same. Every man has been put into the line, even cooks, clerks and drivers. The North Staffs have had a particularly hard time. Even General Penney has been wounded. Shrapnel in the back. General Templer has taken over both the 56th and the 1st Divisions. He will also launch a counter-attack north of the Flyover with the 169th Brigade which has only just landed at Anzio harbour.'

'Templer is a great soldier,' added Major Bridgman. 'Met him once in France. Strong personality. No nonsense. Gets things done fast.'

'Yes we can have every confidence in him,' agreed Colonel Peddie. 'So hang on, Ted, and hope for the best.' They turned and moved on into the darkness.

For three more hours we waited, while an eerie silence made us listen intently and watch every shadow. We had expected renewed shelling at dawn, but at four o'clock while it was bitterly cold and still very dark, came the all-too-familiar flashes in the north, followed by a drumroll of explosions in front of our trenches. Evidently the Germans were about to renew their attack at least two hours before our counter-attack was due to begin.

The barrage lasted half an hour followed by sudden silence, which could only mean that the infantry was on its way. It was too dark to see the murky figures approaching, but our artillery left nothing to chance. The intensive bombardment which thundered from behind us and exploded in a violent eruption in the path of the enemy, seemed so violent that nothing could survive its lethal power.

Nevertheless, a few infantry managed to break through and charge towards us firing as they came. We greeted them with all the firepower we could muster. In the darkness total confusion turned the battlefield into a melee of tracer bullets criss-crossing, mingled with the clatter of Spandaus and Brens, and the haphazard explosion of grenades. Nothing happened quite as expected. (It seldom did in war.) No Germans reached our trenches although several of our men were hit by bullets and shrapnel. The remainder of the night seemed interminable. When at last the dawn first showed in the east, we expected yet another onrush of troops. In our weakened state we would hardly have been able to resist even a diminished attack.

To our astonishment and relief, the German troops came no further. Some lay dead on the sodden earth, others could be seen carrying away their wounded and moving back the way they had come. Our artillery continued to shell the area around Carroceto, but now no fresh waves of infantry came forward to face the shattering blasts. If the Germans had failed in their latest thrust, were they regrouping to launch a new offensive? And when was our counter-attack going to start?

The American General Ernest Harmon, who had arrived on the beach-head a few days earlier, was an ideal leader for attack. Strong and stocky in build, his aggressive nature would brush aside any difficulties. He was now given command of Force H, consisting of the 6th Armoured Infantry Division, and the tanks of the 1st Armoured Division, which was to attack the Germans from the south-east along Bowling Alley. At the same time General Templer, having taken over from the wounded General Penney, commanded Force T to attack north from the Flyover. This Force was to consist mainly of the newly-landed 169th Brigade which would find itself in the thick of the fighting within hours of its arrival; and of course the battle-hardened remains of the 1st Division which were game to the last.

The combined attack was due to start at 11am. The first blow came from the artillery. Eight British artillery regiments combined with eight regiments of Corps artillery put down a co-ordinated barrage of shells on the area to be attacked. Then although Harmon's Force H began to move forward, Templer was aghast to be told that although the 169th Brigade had landed safely, their guns and equipment were still at sea; the Luftwaffe had dropped mines around the harbour entrance, and the port officer had decided to close the port, much to the fury of General Lucas, who immediately countermanded the order, although the ships carrying the guns were now too far out to sea to be recalled in time. Templer decided to launch an attack with tanks alone, but these were unable to advance without infantry support.

By this time Force H had found little initial opposition. Under General Harmon's inspiring leadership the infantry and tanks had started to move forward from behind the Padiglione Woods. Some hours earlier, however, Harmon had received an urgent message from General Lucas to change his plan and converge around the Flyover where another German attack was expected at any moment. Harmon remained adamant: his attack along Bowling Alley, as planned, was essential to prevent the enemy from surging south and cutting us off from the sea.

No sooner had his troops moved off than Harmon was faced with one of the most difficult decisions of his life. An American battalion was reported to be stranded and cut off in the very area where the Allied artillery were to send down the new concentration of shells. Harmon knew that if he cancelled the artillery to save the battalion, his own troops would face far greater casualties; if he postponed the attack, the Germans would have the initiative to attack first and the whole beach-head might be in jeopardy. One way or another some American soldiers might have to be sacrificed. It was the terrible penalty of war.

Harmon did not hesitate: the artillery bombardment must start as planned. His decision was correct. To his intense relief a new message reached him that the battalion (which turned out to be only a platoon) had managed to withdraw during the night and was safe.

Accordingly, an immense barrage was put down, not only by the artillery but by the naval guns pounding the area of Carroceto and the Factory, followed by a deluge of bombs from Allied aircraft. As the barrage lifted, Force H surged forward against strong opposition, establishing a secure front along Bowling Alley. Many German prisoners were captured, all of whom showed signs of battle fatigue, shock and despondency. They had been greatly misled by their own propaganda: the British and American forces were on the point of collapse; only one more push was needed to drive them into the sea and the great and glorious German victory was assured. When they discovered the bitter truth and saw their friends lying dead in the mud, their morale collapsed and many gave themselves up rather than face again the ferocity of the guns and the deadly machine guns.

During the main German offensive, one American regiment, the 157th, had been enduring a lone struggle in the battle of the caves. The whole area, south west of Carroceto, was a confused honeycomb of caves and wadis, which afforded the Germans ideal cover in which to hide troops and infiltrate behind our lines. The commander of the 2nd Battalion of the Regiment, Colonel Brown, skilfully organised the defences so that although the enemy moved secretly by night and cut off their communication, the 2nd Battalion held out for several critical days and nights, preventing the Germans from making an advance in strength. The Battalion was in grave danger, and many wounded need urgent help. At night several carrying parties managed to find their way through the morass of ditches in spite of the enemy machine guns. They brought supplies of food and ammunition, but not nearly enough for the besieged battalion. Water too was in desperately short supply, so they were forced to scoop up contaminated water from the gullies, which they boiled mainly for the thirsty wounded.

General Templer realised their plight and the danger to the beachhead if the enemy finally broke through. He sent the 2/7th Queen's Royal Regiment, which had landed at Anzio only a few hours earlier, forward to relieve them. Unfortunately they soon clashed with a new enemy attack reinforced with a shower of anti-personnel ('butterfly') bombs which caused heavy casualties. The object of the German attack was to engulf and destroy the Americans in the area of the caves. Darkness had now fallen over the battlefield, so there was much confused hand to hand fighting. By midnight the Queen's, under the command of Colonel D. Baynes, had repulsed most of the enemy and brought some little relief to the hard pressed Americans. During the following morning, however, the Germans once again managed to infiltrate through the maze of wadis and ditches and surrounded the caves. That night Colonel Brown decided that his 2nd Battalion would have to break through the German net, aided by covering fire from the Queen's. It was a desperate fight; the men were weak with exhaustion, short of ammunition, struggling through the muddy ground against fierce mortar and machine gun fire. But somehow, against the odds, about two hundred out of the original eight hundred men succeeded and reached the shelter of the main defence line. Of these most were on the point of collapse and nearly starved. Yet they had held the line against the massive German attacks and prevented a serious enemy breakthough.

It was now left to the Queen's to defend the caves and wadis from further German infiltration. The conditions were critical as several badly wounded Americans could not be moved and had to be left behind in the care of their medical officer. A further enemy attack during the morning was repulsed, mainly by artillery fire, but the Germans had encircled the caves with an even tighter stranglehold. C Company of the Queen's found itself completely cut off and short of ammunition. When they were attacked with flamethrowers they were powerless to do anything but surrender. The remaining companies withdrew into the caves, but with little ammunition or food it was impossible to retaliate. When German tanks fired into the entrance to the caves, Colonel Baynes decided they must fight their way out as soon as it was dark. It became a desperate attempt to thrust their way through the encircling Germans. Only Colonel Baynes and about twenty men achieved the impossible. Over 350 officers and men of the Queen's were killed, wounded or captured during this battle of the caves. Yet the combined action of the US 157th Regiment and the 2/7th Queen's had undoubtedly prevented the entire left wing of the beach-head from collapsing.

It then remained for the Irish Guards, who had been sent to fill the gap alongside the caves, to endure a terrible pounding from German infantry and frequent bombing and shelling. For four days the Guards held out in utter misery, with incessant rain, knee-deep floods and mounting casualties so that the area turned into an unbelievable hell. Then at last they were relieved by the 1st Battalion, The Duke of Wellingtons, many of whom were newly joined reinforcements. By now the Germans seemed to have accepted their inability to destroy the defenders, whose power of endurance and resilience astonished them. Their own casualties, mainly from Allied artillery, were mounting at an alarming rate.

Thus stalemate caused a kind of paralysis over the whole beach-head. The appalling weather prevented tanks from churning through the thick mud, while the aircraft could not attack through the low clouds. It was during this partial lull that General Clarke, under pressure from both Churchill and Alexander, decided to replace General Lucas and appointed General Truscott to take command over the beach-head forces. Truscott was a man with a high reputation as a strict disciplinarian, with an aggressive manner intensified by his husky voice, and an unshakeable belief in victory. His appointment brought new vigour into the higher command, and his well-known bravery under fire was an inspiration to all. Unlike Lucas who had commanded the beach-head from a bunker in Nettuno, Truscott believed in being with the frontline troops in the thick of the battle, spurring them on when things appeared bad. So the whole attitude of Corps HQ was revolutionised as their new commander planned not for defence but for victory.

In contrast a very different attitude prevailed in the mountains of Berchtesgaden. Hitler had been waiting daily for news of the great German victory in Italy. His soldiers must be invincible, so any reports of failure were slanderous on their reputation. Kesselring now realised that Hitler must be warned that a further all-out offensive was no longer possible. His Army Group had fought to a standstill over nearly six weeks and had been held at the last line of resistance. Kesselring's Chief of Staff, General Siegfried Westphal, was chosen to be the messenger of ill-tidings and to try to make Hitler realise the appalling conditions his troops were enduring. Westphal was a man of good education and intellect, with a fine military record. If anyone could convince Hitler it was he. Expecting to be shouted at by an enraged Hitler, Westphal explained the background and progress of the war in Italy, and how their offensive had been halted mainly by the stupendous artilley bombardments and naval gunfire, the Allied air supremacy and the powerful infantry. Hitler surprisingly listened intently while Westphal spoke for three hours. Instead of his usual hysterics, the Führer seemed calm but crestfallen. All he wanted, he said, was just one great German victory. After that his secret weapons and the supreme German army would ensure that they would vanquish the Allies, and the Wehrmacht would triumph. Kesselring must make one more attempt to crush the Allies, one more blitzkrieg to drive fiercely through the defensive ring and storm forward to the sea.

So it was that on 29 February 1944, the Germans began their final, last-hope attack while the rain poured down, turning the already sodden terrain into a watery morass.

8
'My Turn Next?'

Our waterlogged trenches became more unpleasant every day. Above all we longed for sleep, but there was no chance while the rain continued and unpredictable shells might land anywhere at any moment of the day or night. Although the main offensive appeared to have ended, the enemy kept up a continual pressure by sending strong fighting patrols against our positions. These often inflicted severe casualties as they swarmed upon us during the night, spraying our trenches with Spandaus, and hurling grenades at close range. We responded with every available weapon, usually decimating their numbers, yet still they came. We, in contrast, were sent not in large fighting patrols, but in small recce patrols to listen, observe and report back with information. Nearly every night I with two or three men set off into the darkness. By now, after much practice, we found our way silently, moving from one dark shadow to another, like Indians on a trail, avoiding yet noting enemy movements, and bringing back reports to add to Battalion intelligence.

It had now become a war of attrition and endurance. At any moment a shell, grenade or bullet might put an end to one's activity. The unspoken and unavoidable question was 'will it be my turn next?'

The days seemed interminable; we were getting nowhere and without news of what was to happen next. The long expected breakthrough of the Fifth Army at Cassino had still not happened. The news had not reached us that a few days earlier, on the 15th February, some 450 tons of bombs had been dropped by waves of B-17 bombers on the Benedictine Abbey of Monte Cassino. Yet what was devised as a final knockout blow, turned out to be a useless and tragic devastation which served no military purpose, and gave the Germans a propaganda coup. At the time of the bombing there had been no adequate coordination with the ground forces, and the infantry attack by the 4th Indian Division did not take place until three days later, by which time the Germans had prepared new defences in the rubble of the

Abbey. The only advantage to the Allies was the psychological relief to the forces surrounding Monte Cassino that the Germans would no longer be able to use the Abbey as an all-seeing observation post. It was said that not even a mouse could move without the spotter in the Abbey honing on to it. The Abbey itself had become a symbol of the Germans' power over the entire area. In retrospect two aspects of the tragedy of Cassino must be mentioned: the cooperation between the different Allied nations – Britain, Canada, New Zealand, India, Poland, France and the Gurkhas – was remarkable and greatly added to the ultimate success. Also the bravery and fortitude of the troops on both sides was beyond praise. The Allied troops fought in dreadful, terrifying conditions over many months while the Germans – particularly the 1st Parachute Division – was later described by General Alexander: 'The tenacity of these German Paratroops is quite remarkable, considering that they were subjected to the whole Mediterranean Air Force plus the better part of 800 guns under greatest concentration of fire-power which has ever been put down and lasting for six hours. I doubt if there are any other troops in the world who could have stood up to it and then gone on fighting with the ferocity they have.'*

It was not until 18 May, that the 4th British Division finally captured Cassino, and the Poles ran up their red and white flag over the rubble that once was the Monastery.†

While we still knew nothing of the tragic events at Cassino, it became clear by 29 February, that the Germans were beginning a new devastating offensive. The warning came at dawn with a sudden artillery bombardment all along the line. No doubt the fighting patrols had been in preparation for this by probing our positions to ascertain the weakest point. So once again we were forced to shelter at the bottom of our slit trenches and wait in hope. When the bombardment lifted the sounds of an intense artillery attack came from some distance away to the right of the Flyover. We waited tensely in case it would come our way, but instead we watched as squadrons of Spitfires zoomed overhead and dived down towards the German forces.

*Churchill: *Second World War*, Vol V, p 449
† Several miracles were said to have occurred during the bombing and also later with the reconstruction and restoration of the Abbey and its works of art. It was completely rebuilt with funds from the Italian and American Governments, and consecrated by Pope Paul in 1964. It now stands as a building of unique beauty and sanctity, with the original coat of arms: 'Succisa virescit' (Cut down it lives again).

Then another wave of planes flying very low roared towards us. Someone shouted, 'Heads down! They're Messerschmidts!' At the same moment came the rattle of machine guns as they began to strafe our positions.

Suddenly I heard a loud cry. The next moment I realised that it was I who had shouted. Looking down at my leg I saw a stain of red welling from a tear in my trousers at the top of my thigh. The usual cry for stretcher bearers went up, and almost before I realised what was happening Gordon had arrived and was removing my trousers to apply a shell dressing. There were two large gashes in the flesh where the Messerschmidt's bullet had torn right through the leg. All the planes had now vanished and our part of the front was for the moment quiet. Major Bridgman arrived to see what was happening. He looked down into my trench and waved a greeting. 'Hi,' he smiled, 'now you'll have to eat your breakfast off the mantlepiece!' Then lighting a cigarette for me he insisted on me smoking it. Just as Gordon was finishing the dressing, Colonel Peddie appeared while on a tour of the Battalion.

'Hello Ted,' he exclaimed. 'What the hell are you doing down there?'

'He had a quarrel with one of those Messerschmidts,' explained Major Bridgman.

'They seem to have taken the pants off you all right,' said James Peddie.

'Not for long,' I replied as Gordon drew up my trousers again, and helped to lift me onto the waiting stretcher. Sergeant Maclaren arrived, put my pack onto the stretcher and helped to make me comfortable. As the stretcher bearers lifted me onto their shoulders, James Peddie and Lindsay Bridgman shook hands with me, wishing me luck. Several other men ran up to shake hands and make some parting joke. 'Good luck, sir. Don't stay away long.' 'See you in Rome, sir!' The last thing I saw of these muddy, weather-beaten men, they were all smiling. Lindsay waved his steel helmet to me and then turned to ensure his Company was ready to deal with the Germans.

I wondered anxiously how strong would be the enemy attack. Sergeant Maclaren would, I knew, expertly take over 10 Platoon, but already I felt a kind of pull, urging me to be back with the men I knew so well. Little did I know at that time that the Battalion would continue fighting on this dreadful beach-head for four more months and be the first attacking wave to assault the Alban Hills and on the 6th June to be part of the force to capture Rome. Of the original Battalion only a few would remain. But Private Gordon who was now carrying me back to the Regimental Aid Post would be one of those few. In over a year from now he would still be fetching in the wounded from battles in the snowcovered mountains of the north.

After the first numbing shock, the pain in my leg swiftly increased. A few stray shells landed nearby while I was being carried across the mile of rough country to the Aid Post. Doc McIntosh greeted me as though he had long been expecting me, and an orderly gave me a heaven-sent mug of hot sweet tea. After that I lost track of what happened. I must have been in and out of the operating theatre, because I found myself still on a stretcher but down in a slit trench. As I was coming to, a loud crash shattered the flimsy building. A man who had evidently been hit by shrapnel fell down on top of my leg, which did not improve its condition. He was quickly lifted out, whether dead or only wounded I was not told. The episode proved yet again how every inch of the beach-head was under constant shellfire, from which there was no escape.

The next few days passed in a blur; my main recollection was being permanently thirsty and frequently calling out for water. But as more and more men were brought in, the orderlies were under great pressure. Eventually I was told that a tank landing craft had been ordered to evacuate the wounded from the beach-head and would sail from Anzio harbour that night.

My next memory is of lying on the deck of a ship gliding slowly into Naples harbour as the sun was rising over the mountains. When the ship changed course, an amazing sight came into view. From the cone of Vesuvius voluminous billows of smoke and black clouds were rising into the sky. Lurid flashes and fiery eruptions were angrily clashing against a background of molten lava slowly eating its way down the mountain side. The smell of sulphur wafted across the bay and made breathing difficult. Soon the rising sun was hidden behind the fulminations engulfing the volcano, now in its first major eruption since 1929. The tremendous power of nature far exceeded the warring struggles of men. Later a report to the Naval Commander-in-Chief stated, 'The Naples group of ports is now discharging at the rate of twelve million tons a year, while Vesuvius is estimated to be doing thirty million *a day*. We can but admire this gesture of the gods.'

The awe-inspiring sight of the volcano, which as the hours passed thrust even greater mountains of smoke and ash into the sky, made a fitting background to my departure from the battlefield. My turn had come and I was still alive.

The bay was soon entangled with all manner of ships awaiting their turn to enter the harbour, but about midday the ship I was in managed to dock. I was quickly taken to hospital in Naples and a week later flown to a less busy hospital in Catania.

Yet in my confused dreams I had to find my way back to my platoon where the men were all waiting. James Peddie was about to send me and a few men on another night patrol, and Lindsay Bridgman waiting to cheer us on our return. Sergeant Maclaren, Corporals Tripney and Boyes stood as resolute as ever as bombs fell around us. But dreams often became nightmares. I heard the men calling while machine guns clattered incessantly, and it was impossible for me to reach them through the impenetrable darkness.

Then after a few days, I was in the next bed to the Guards officer, whose story, already related, helped to restore my mind to the present. I was able to look hopefully to the future, to the end of the war and to peace. The world after the war would surely have a new vision, free from strife. Then with Rupert Brooke I imagined,

> Honour has come back, as a King, to earth,
> And paid his subjects with a royal wage;
> And Nobleness walks in our ways again;
> And we have come into our heritage.

Epilogue

The final German offensive began as expected on 29 February. Once again both sides suffered severe casualties, particularly from artillery bombardments. This time however, the Germans having experienced the overwhelming fire power of the Allies, showed less of the ferocity and aggression that had made them such fearsome foes. At certain places they managed to dent the defenders' positions, but after two days' fighting they had made no significant progress.

Then on 2 March the clouds lifted and a massive air attack was launched by hundreds of Fortresses, Liberators, Lightnings and Thunderbolts. The effect was more appalling for the Germans than anything they had ever experienced. Nowhere was safe; no shelter could be found from the terrible torrent of death from the skies.

Kesselring and von Mackensen realised that they had reached the end of their resources; no more large scale attacks were possible. Hitler, preoccupied with losses on the Russian front, lost interest in Italy, although later blamed his losses in Russia to the need to keep so many divisions tied up in Italy.

There followed two months of small-scale fighting, mainly at battalion and platoon level. It was a time of sheer misery for the troops in the front line, and boredom combined with the risk of being shelled for those supposed to be in 'rest' areas.

As reinforcements arrived for the 6th Gordons, a number of changes were made. Although Colonel James Peddie remained for some months yet, his second in command, Major J L Baucher left to command the London Irish. Major Jim Williamson, who had carried out the lone patrol behind enemy lines on the night of Horror Farm, handed over as Adjutant to Captain Temple Nimmo, in order to take command of a newly formed D Company. Major Leslie Hatt became commander of C Company, formed entirely from reinforcements newly arrived from Britain. This was a very responsible position as both NCOs and men had to adapt remarkably quickly to the arduous beach-head conditions. They soon came under heavy shelling, which caused the death of a young lieutenant as soon as he arrived and wounded another.

George Reynolds-Payne, who had been detached from B Company to carry out special duties with Battalion HQ was severely wounded by an anti-personnel bomb. His departure caused great regrets among his many friends. When times were at their worst one could always rely on George to enliven, cheer and encourage inspite of all that the Germans could throw at us. One of his friends said, 'When I go to Heaven I shall say I'm a friend of George and that will be the Open Sesame to the Pearly Gates.'

After George had left, several other officers joined the Battalion as reinforcements, including Captain Crawford from the Capetown Highlanders. He was a father figure to the sixteen other officers from the same South African Regiment.

Of the old stagers who remained was Robin Bain of the Carrier Platoon, who had played a major role as a mobile force in both defence and attack. He referred to himself as a Scottish cattle drover, but after the war he gave his daughter a castle in Scotland as a wedding present, and was always equally generous to the men in his platoon.

After my sudden departure from the battlefield, 10 platoon was taken over by Stewart Ross, a territorial officer, and like me a solicitor. Fortunately he remained to be part of the break-through to Rome and later during the period of training for mountain warfare. As he later wrote to me, 'You can imagine how useful this was when our next role found us in the streets of Florence! 10 Platoon was once again the leading platoon as we crossed the Ponte Veccio. Florence was a peculiar part of the campaign, mostly involving patrolling within the city in areas sometimes held by the Partisans and sometimes by the German Airborne or Mountain Divisions. (Florence seems to have had a fascination for troops trained in mountain warfare.) Some of the platoon were wounded in Florence, and some were lost in the Monte Grande sector.'

It was not until 11 May that the battle for the break out from the beach-head finally began. A skilful strategic plan had been worked out by General Alexander. First he managed to deceive the Germans into thinking that no major Allied attacks would begin until June at the earliest, and that before then a new amphibious landing would be made north-west of Rome. The main object of Alexander's plan was not the capture of Rome, which was of course incidental, but to surround, capture or destroy the German forces amounting to twenty German divisions.

According to the plan, the Allied forces in the beach-head, amounting to six divisions were to start their major offensive on 11 May. At the same time the 8th Army were to attack along the Liri Valley, capture Cassino and advance towards Rome. The 5th Army were to advance along Route 7 and also converge towards Rome. The three attacks would completely cut off the German forces and prevent their retreat and subsequent regrouping in North Italy.

To begin with the three pronged attack went exactly as planned. The German 10th Army was forced to withdraw. General Truscott's American forces succeeded brilliantly and were swarming north to cut off the retreating German army when General Mark Clarke made the surprising decision to countermand Alexander's orders. He ordered Truscott to change direction and make for Rome so that the Americans should have the honour of being the first troops to enter the city. The unfortunate result of this was that the German 10th Army escaped unmolested to the north, and Alexander's order for the destruction of the enemy in Italy could not fully be realised for a whole year.

Nevertheless, General Alexander's great strategic skills both in North Africa and Italy were fully recognised, not only by Churchill but also by Eisenhower who called him 'the ace card in the British Empire's hand', and by Bradley who thought him 'the outstanding general's general of the European war, who brought to his command the reasonableness and patience and modesty of a great soldier'.

The 6th Gordons played a very active part in the battles leading to the breakout from the beach-head and the advance to Rome. In particular, on 30 May, after patrols had been sent out before dawn, the Battalion successfully attacked a strong German force. In spite of a number of casualties they reached and secured all their objectives. When a platoon of C Company lost its commander and half of the men, Sergeant G. Morton took over and by his personal example held the remainder of the platoon together all that afternoon and evening in an isolated and precarious position, until the enemy withdrew. Private W. Pickard, a stretcher brearer, also of C Company, took care of the wounded without relief and heedless of the danger, over a period of nine critical hours. As Colonel Peddie reported, 'Today was a triumph for the Battalion. The men who have marched in the heat and dust since 28th May impressed everyone with their cheerfulness and determination.'

By 4 June the Battalion had reached an area 10 miles south of Rome. The only reason they had to wait before entering the city was to allow the Americans the privilege of being first. However, by 8 June the pipes marched through Rome and were given a great welcome by cheering Roman crowds.

Subsequently the Battalion moved into the Alban Hills, now mercifully cleared of German artillery, for further training in mountain warfare, and in July they carried out river crossing practice across the Tiber.

On 30 July HM King George VI came to inspect the troops. This was a moving and joyful occasion, and a fitting climax to the Anzio campaign. The Battalion lined the route taken by the royal car as the King was given a rousing and enthusiastic welcome.

In due course of time the 6th Gordon Highlanders were awarded Battle Honours for the part they played on the Anzio beach-head.

In 1948 a memorial for the fallen was erected at Anzio by Colonel James Peddie. The Battle Exploits Memorials Committee described the Battalion's actions in the following terms:

> The Sixth Gordons were one of the first two battalions to assault the Anzio beaches, and they fought in the beaches throughout until the capture of Rome by the beach-head forces on 5 June 1944. During these four and a half months the Battalion suffered severe casualties, including a large number of officers and men who had served with the Battalion since 1940. In addition to leading the assault on the beaches on 22 January, the Battalion put up a most stubborn resistance to the first of the series of enemy counter attacks against the British forces. On 4 February, the obstinacy of the Battalion was largely instrumental in rendering possible the evacuation of the 3rd Infantry Brigade who were virtually cut off. The Battalion continued to fight on for the next four months in the restricted area of the beach-head until the British forces broke out at the end of May.

The Perilous Road had at last, after many trials, led to Rome.

*In Remembrance of all those
who fought for their Country.*

THE GORDON HIGHLANDERS

BATTLE HONOURS

Regimental Colour – Mysore, Seringapatam, Egmont-op-Zee, Mandora, Corunna, Fuentes d'Onor, Almaraz, Vittoria, Pyrenees, Nive, Orthes, Peninsula, Waterloo, South Africa 1835, Delhi 1857, Lucknow, Charasiah, Kabul 1879, Kandahar 1880, Afghanistan 1878-80, Tel-el-Kebir, Egypt 1882, 1884, Nile 1884-5, Chitral, Tirah, Defence of Ladysmith, Paardeberg, South Africa 1899-1902.

Queen's Colour – Mons, Le Cateau, Marne 1914-18, Ypres 1914-15-17, Loos, Somme 1916-18, Ancre 1916, Arras 1917-18, Cambrai 1917-18, Vittorio–Veneto, Odon, Reichswald, Goch, Rhine, North West Europe, 1940 '44-45, El Alamein, Mareth, North Africa 1942-43, Sferro, Anzio.

Index

Abbey, Cassino 158
Afrika Korps 5, 28, 47
Alexander, General, Sir Harold 12, 38-40, 80, 89, 90; award by Churchill 67; 163-4
Algiers 5
Allardice, L/Corporal 32, 109, 141
Anderson, General KN 38, 39
Anderson, Major, VC, of the Argylls 30
Anzio Annie 119
Anzio 77; landing at 80-4; harbour mined 152
Argyll & Sutherland Highlanders 29
Arnim, General von 5, 12, 37, 40; captured 47
Arabs 48, 55, 57, 69
Artillery, Royal 65, 143, 152

Bain, Capt R 25, 26, 112, 163
Battle Exploits Memorial Committee 165
Baynes, Col D, QRR 154-5
BBC Home and Overseas Service 72
Bizerta 39, 43, 46, 69
Bou Aoukaz 29 *et seq*, 41
Boyes, Corporal 19, 23, 32, 33, 90, 92, 141
Bradley, General Omar 12, 39, 66
Bridgman, Major Lindsay 13, 14, 18, 23, 24, 26, 34, 61, 77, 93, 107, 112, 128, 134; in catacombs 139
Brigade, 3rd 34, 35
Brown, Colonel (US) 154
Butterfly Bombs 32, 154

Campoleone 93-5
Canaris, Admiral 84, 89
Capri, Isle of 79
Carroceto 95-7
Casablanca (Churchill–Roosevelt) 4
Cassino, Monte 5, 77, 88; bombing Abbey 157; 164

Castellammare 76
Chouat, capture of 44
Churchill, Winston 4, 67; plans campaign 78; 'Wild cat' message 86, 89, 90
Churchill tanks 14, 27
Coningham, Air Vice Marshal Sir Arthur 39
Clarke, General Mark 88, 145, 150, 164
Craig, Pte, Bren Gunner 23, 25, 141
Crawford, Captain, Cape Town Highlanders 163
Crewdson, John, Lieut 47
Cunningham, Sir Andrew, Admiral of the Fleet 39, 80, 88

Darby Rangers 84; battle for Cisterna 124
Deboys, Norman, Lieut 70, 113, 131
D'Este, Carlo, Military historian 119
Derbyshire Yeomanry 46
Divisions: 1st 16, 30, 39, 47, 48, 49, 64, 139, 145, 152; 4th 47, 158; 5th 88; 7th Armoured 38, 39, 42, 46, 47; 50th & 51st 37, 39; 56th 139; 78th 29; French 39, 43; Indian 37, 38, 39, 157; New Zealand 5, 37-9
Djerbel Jaffa 7, 9, 12
Djerbel Ressas 64
Djerbel Tahent, US attack 43
Duke of Wellingtons 35, 66, 104, 108, 155

Eagles, General, (US) 139
East Surrey Regt 7, 8
Eighth Army 38, 48
Eisenhower, General Dwight D 38; Victory parade 48, 65, 66; at Carthage with Churchill 86
El Guettar 12
Engineers, Royal 65

167

Factory, The 95
Fifth Army 87
Fitzgerald, Major Irish Guards 103
Fleming, Major 31
Florence, 6th Gordons in 163
Flyover, The 95, 145, 147
Forbes, Major 24, 25
French Afrique Corps 43

Garioch, H, Lieut 122
George VI, King 3, 10, 73, 165
Ghardimau 55
Gordon Highlanders, 6th Battalion 5, 7, 30, 43, 164; Victory March 47, 65; at Pantelleria 49; Victory parade – Eisenhower 65; at Salerno 75; at Horror Farm 105 *et seq*; Loss of A, C, D Coys 117, 122; Battle Honours 165
Gordon Lennox, Lt Col 98-9
Gräser Battle Group 149
Grenadier Guards 30, 95 *et seq*, 123
Gugel Dr (German hospital) 56, 60
Gustav Line 77, 88

Hammamet 47, 64
Hargreaves, Lieut, Gren. Guards 95
Harmon, General Ernest (US) 146, 152-3
Hatt, Leslie, Major 24, 25, 162
Haw Haw, Lord 56
Hermann Goering Division 16, 84, 125
Highland, 51st Division 37, 39
Hitler, Adolf 28, 86, 91, 127, 156, 162
Hoffman, Dr 45, 55, 58
Hohler, Capt, Gren. Guards 99
Holwell, L/Cpl, Irish Guards 102
Horrocks, General Sir Brian 38, 41
Hussars, Eleventh 46

Indian Divisions 37-9, 157
Irish Guards 30 *et seq*, 100 *et seq*, 155
Italians 107; capitulation 75

Kesselring, Field Marshal Albert 75, 84; reacts to invasion 88, 91; final plan 138, 156
Kesserine Pass 12
Kings Shropshire Light Infantry 35, 66, 104, 108

La Calle fishing village 61
Leckie, James, signals officer 72, 121; killed 142
'Lillie Marlene' 67
London Scottish 120
Longstop 5, 8, 28, 29
Loyal Regiment 18, 26, 146, 149
Lucas, General John 84, 90, 139, 153, 155
Luftwaffe 40, 85, 91, 138, 144

Maclaren, Sergeant 23, 24, 25, 32, 90, 141; wounded 32, 52; takes over platoon 159
McIntosh, Dr 26, 27, 120, 160
McCreery, General Richard, 5th Div 88
Mackensen, General von 84, 138, 149
Malta, siege of 49, 67
Mareth Line 37
Martin, Stanley, Lieut 26
Medjerda River 28, 29, 47
Medjez el Bab 5
Messerschmidts 25, 144, 159
Minefields 26-7
Momper, Dr (German hospital) 56
Monastir 48, 55
Montgomery, General Bernard 5, 37 *et seq*, 43
Moore, Brigadier, 2nd Brigade 44, 76-7
Moran, Lord 86
Murray, Brigadier ASP, Guards Brigade 95
Mussolini, Benito 49, 50, 70, 89

Naples 76, 160
Navy Royal 38, combined exercises 75
Nazi 'New Order' 59
Needham, Lieut, Gren. Guards 97
New Zealand Div 5, 37-9, 158
North Staffordshire Regt 26, 151
Nimmo, Capt Temple 162

Operation Shingle 86
Overlord 4

Padaglione 129
Padaglione Woods 139, 142
Padre 53, 57, 72
Pantalleria 49
Pantano Ditch 124
Panzers 84, 88

168

Panzer divisions 12, 37, 47, 75, 78, 95, 125, 149
Parker, Pte 9, 11, 14
Patton, General George 12, 43, 66
Peddie, Colonel James 8, 10, 12, 17, 28, 43, 73, 92, 93, 121, 162
Penney, General W 10, 65, 145; wounded 151
Pipes and Drums 73, 165
Prisoners of war, German 55

Queen's Royal Regiment 154-5

Rae, Major 25, 31
RAF, bombing by 35, 38, 41, 49, 145, 162
Rangers (see US and Darby Rangers)
RASC, RAMC, REME 66
Reay, batman 14, 24, 32, 141
Reconnaissance Regiment 129
Reynolds-Payne, Capt George 70, 163
Rommel, Field Marshal Erwin 5, 37 *et seq*
Roosevelt, Franklin D, President 4, 86
Ross, Stewart 163

Salerno 75
Scots Guards 101 *et seq*
St Dunstans 69
Sengler, General F von 88
Sharnhorst sunk 87
Shingle, Operation 86
Sherman Tanks 114 *et seq*, 122
Sherwood Forresters 35, 66
Sicily 49, 70
Sidney, Major WP, VC (Lord D'Lisle and Dudley) 123 *et seq*
Signals, Royal Corps of 65
Sinclair, Major 20, 21
Sinclair, Pte, dash for ambulance 136
Smith R, Capt (later Brigadier) 25

Solomon, recital in Tunis 67
Spinazzola 70, 73
Spitfires 89, 138, 158
Stewart-Richardson, Major, Irish Guards 103
Stukas 52, 54

Taranto 70
Tedder, Air Chief Marshal Sir Arthur 39, 87
Templer, General Sir Gerald (later Field Marshal) 139, 151, 152
Tiger tanks 21, 116, 117, 122, 134, 143
Tripney, Corporal 9, 10, 23, 32, 33, 53, 141, 147
Truscott, General LJ 83, 124, 155, 164
Tunis 12, 46, 48, 67

U-Boats 3
US Forces: Armoured 37, 39, 47, 152; Force H 153; 2nd Corps 43, 88; 6th Corps 83-4; Infantry Divisions 37, 39, 139; Rangers 5, 77, 84; 157 Regt 154-5; Regimental Combat Teams 143, 145

Vesuvius 76; eruption 160-1
V1 and V2 rockets 86
Victory 47
Victory parade 64
Vogel, Dr (German hospital) 58

Wadi Akarit 37
Watson, Pte 23, 141
Wedderburn, Lieut, Gren. Guards 99, 100
Westphal, General Siegfried 90; warns Hitler 156
West Kents, Royal 29
Williamson, James, Major, sole patrol behind enemy lines 118 *et seq*, 162